MAX LUCADO

LIFE LESSONS *from*

1 CORINTHIANS

A Spiritual Health Check-Up

PREPARED BY THE LIVINGSTONE CORPORATION

THOMAS NELSON
Since 1798

Life Lessons from 1 Corinthians

© 2018 by Max Lucado

Published in Nashville, Tennessee, by Thomas Nelson. Thomas Nelson is a registered trademark of HarperCollins Christian Publishing, Inc.

Produced with the assistance of the Livingstone Corporation. Project staff include Jake Barton, Joel Bartlett, Andy Culbertson, Mary Horner Collins, and Will Reaves.

Editor: Neil Wilson

All Scripture quotations, unless otherwise indicated, are taken from *The Holy Bible, New International Version*®, NIV®. Copyright © 1973, 1978, 1984, 2011 by Biblica, Inc.™ Used by permission. All rights reserved worldwide.

Scripture quotations marked NKJV are taken from the New King James Version®. Copyright © 1982 by Thomas Nelson. Used by permission. All rights reserved.

Scripture quotations marked TLB are taken from The Living Bible, copyright © 1971. Used by permission of Tyndale House Publishers, Inc., Carol Stream, Illinois 60188. All Rights Reserved.

Material for the "Inspiration" sections taken from the following books:

A Gentle Thunder. Copyright © 1995 by Max Lucado. Thomas Nelson, a registered trademark of HarperCollins Christian Publishing, Inc., Nashville, Tennessee.

God Came Near. Copyright © 2004 by Max Lucado. Thomas Nelson, a registered trademark of HarperCollins Christian Publishing, Inc., Nashville, Tennessee.

The Great House of God. Copyright © 1997 by Max Lucado. Thomas Nelson, a registered trademark of HarperCollins Christian Publishing, Inc., Nashville, Tennessee.

It's Not About Me. Copyright © 2004 by Max Lucado. Thomas Nelson, a registered trademark of HarperCollins Christian Publishing, Inc., Nashville, Tennessee.

Just Like Jesus. Copyright © 2003 by Max Lucado. Thomas Nelson, a registered trademark of HarperCollins Christian Publishing, Inc., Nashville, Tennessee.

A Love Worth Giving. Copyright 2002 by Max Lucado. Thomas Nelson, a registered trademark of HarperCollins Christian Publishing, Inc., Nashville, Tennessee.

Max on Life. Copyright © 2010 by Max Lucado. Thomas Nelson, a registered trademark of HarperCollins Christian Publishing, Inc., Nashville, Tennessee.

More to Your Story. Copyright © 2011, 2016 by Max Lucado. Thomas Nelson, a registered trademark of HarperCollins Christian Publishing, Inc., Nashville, Tennessee.

No Wonder They Call Him the Savior. Copyright © 1986, 2004 by Max Lucado. Thomas Nelson, a registered trademark of HarperCollins Christian Publishing, Inc., Nashville, Tennessee.

Traveling Light. Copyright © 2001 by Max Lucado. Thomas Nelson, a registered trademark of HarperCollins Christian Publishing, Inc., Nashville, Tennessee.

When God Whispers Your Name. Copyright © 1994, 1999 by Max Lucado. Thomas Nelson, a registered trademark of HarperCollins Christian Publishing, Inc., Nashville, Tennessee.

Thomas Nelson titles may be purchased in bulk for educational, business, fundraising, or sales promotional use. For information, please e-mail SpecialMarkets@ThomasNelson.com.

ISBN 978-0-310-08642-0

First Printing May 2018 / Printed in the United States of America

CONTENTS

How to Study the Bible   v

Introduction to the Book of 1 Corinthians   ix

Lesson 1   The Folly of Human Wisdom (*1 Corinthians 1:18–31*)   1

Lesson 2   God's Wisdom Revealed (*1 Corinthians 2:6–16*)   11

Lesson 3   Work That Lasts (*1 Corinthians 3:3–15*)   21

Lesson 4   Serving Christ (*1 Corinthians 4:6–19*)   31

Lesson 5   Self-Sacrifice (*1 Corinthians 9:16–22*)   41

Lesson 6   Temptation (*1 Corinthians 10:1–13*)   51

Lesson 7   Liberty and Love (*1 Corinthians 10:23–33*)   61

Lesson 8   Spiritual Gifts (*1 Corinthians 12:1–11*)   71

Lesson 9   The Body of Christ (*1 Corinthians 12:12–26*)   81

Lesson 10   True Love (*1 Corinthians 13:1–13*)   91

Lesson 11   Christ's Victory Over Death (*1 Corinthians 15:20–34*) 101

Lesson 12   Giving to God's Work (*1 Corinthians 16:1–11*)   111

Leader's Guide for Small Groups   121

CONTENTS

HOW TO STUDY THE BIBLE

The Bible is a peculiar book. Words crafted in another language. Deeds done in a distant era. Events recorded in a far-off land. Counsel offered to a foreign people. It is a peculiar book.

It's surprising that anyone reads it. It's too old. Some of its writings date back 5,000 years. It's too bizarre. The book speaks of incredible floods, fires, earthquakes, and people with supernatural abilities. It's too radical. The Bible calls for undying devotion to a carpenter who called himself God's Son.

Logic says this book shouldn't survive. Too old, too bizarre, too radical.

The Bible has been banned, burned, scoffed, and ridiculed. Scholars have mocked it as foolish. Kings have branded it as illegal. A thousand times over the grave has been dug and the dirge has begun, but somehow the Bible never stays in the grave. Not only has it survived, but it has also thrived. It is the single most popular book in all of history. It has been the bestselling book in the world for years!

There is no way on earth to explain it. Which perhaps is the only explanation. For the Bible's durability is not found on *earth* but in *heaven*. The millions who have tested its claims and claimed its promises know there is but one answer: the Bible is God's book and God's voice.

As you read it, you would be wise to give some thought to two questions: *What is the purpose of the Bible?* and *How do I study the Bible?* Time spent reflecting on these two issues will greatly enhance your Bible study.

What is the purpose of the Bible?

Let the Bible itself answer that question: *"From infancy you have known the Holy Scriptures, which are able to make you wise for salvation through faith in Christ Jesus"* (2 Timothy 3:15).

The purpose of the Bible? Salvation. God's highest passion is to get his children home. His book, the Bible, describes his plan of salvation. The purpose of the Bible is to proclaim God's plan and passion to save his children.

This is the reason why this book has endured through the centuries. It dares to tackle the toughest questions about life: *Where do I go after I die? Is there a God? What do I do with my fears?* The Bible is the treasure map that leads to God's highest treasure—eternal life.

But how do you study the Bible? Countless copies of Scripture sit unread on bookshelves and nightstands simply because people don't know how to read it. What can you do to make the Bible real in your life?

The clearest answer is found in the words of Jesus: *"Ask and it will be given to you; seek and you will find; knock and the door will be opened to you"* (Matthew 7:7).

The first step in understanding the Bible is asking God to help you. You should read it prayerfully. If anyone understands God's Word, it is because of God and not the reader.

"The Advocate, the Holy Spirit, whom the Father will send in my name, will teach you all things and will remind you of everything I have said to you" (John 14:26).

Before reading the Bible, pray and invite God to speak to you. Don't go to Scripture looking for your idea, but go searching for his.

Not only should you read the Bible prayerfully, but you should also read it carefully. *"Seek and you will find"* is the pledge. The Bible is not a newspaper to be skimmed but rather a mine to be quarried. *"If you look for it as for silver and search for it as for hidden treasure, then you will understand the fear of the LORD and find the knowledge of God"* (Proverbs 2:4–5).

Any worthy find requires effort. The Bible is no exception. To understand the Bible, you don't have to be brilliant, but you must be willing to roll up your sleeves and search.

"Do your best to present yourself to God as one approved, a worker who does not need to be ashamed and who correctly handles the word of truth" (2 Timothy 2:15).

Here's a practical point. Study the Bible a bit at a time. Hunger is not satisfied by eating twenty-one meals in one sitting once a week. The body needs a steady diet to remain strong. So does the soul. When God sent food to his people in the wilderness, he didn't provide loaves already made. Instead, he sent them manna in the shape of *"thin flakes like frost on the ground"* (Exodus 16:14).

God gave manna in limited portions.

God sends spiritual food the same way. He opens the heavens with just enough nutrients for today's hunger. He provides *"a rule for this, a rule for that; a little here, a little there"* (Isaiah 28:10).

Don't be discouraged if your reading reaps a small harvest. Some days a lesser portion is all that is needed. What is important is to search every day for that day's message. A steady diet of God's Word over a lifetime builds a healthy soul and mind.

It's much like the little girl who returned from her first day at school feeling a bit dejected. Her mom asked, "Did you learn anything?"

"Apparently not enough," the girl responded. "I have to go back tomorrow, and the next day, and the next . . . "

Such is the case with learning. And such is the case with Bible study. Understanding comes little by little over a lifetime.

There is a third step in understanding the Bible. After the asking and seeking comes the knocking. After you ask and search, *"knock and the door will be opened to you"* (Matthew 7:7).

To knock is to stand at God's door. To make yourself available. To climb the steps, cross the porch, stand at the doorway, and volunteer. Knocking goes beyond the realm of thinking and into the realm of acting.

To knock is to ask, *What can I do? How can I obey? Where can I go?*

It's one thing to know what to do. It's another to do it. But for those who do it—those who choose to obey—a special reward awaits them.

"Whoever looks intently into the perfect law that gives freedom, and continues in it—not forgetting what they have heard, but doing it—they will be blessed in what they do" (James 1:25).

What a promise. Blessings come to those who do what they read in God's Word! It's the same with medicine. If you only read the label but ignore the pills, it won't help. It's the same with food. If you only read the recipe but never cook, you won't be fed. And it's the same with the Bible. If you only read the words but never obey, you'll never know the joy God has promised.

Ask. Search. Knock. Simple, isn't it? So why don't you give it a try? If you do, you'll see why the Bible is the most remarkable book in history.

INTRODUCTION TO
The Book of
1 Corinthians

A man was walking up a mountain when he heard a voice. "Carry me with you," it requested.

The man turned and saw a snake. He refused. "If I carry you up the mountain, you will bite me."

"I wouldn't do that," the snake assured. "All I need is some help. I am slow, and you are fast. Please be kind and carry me to the top of the mountain."

It was against the man's better judgment, but he agreed. He picked up the snake, put it in his shirt, and resumed the journey. When the man reached the top, he reached in his shirt to remove the snake and got bit. He fell to the ground, and the snake slithered away.

"You lied!" the man cried. "You said you wouldn't bite me!"

The snake stopped and looked back. "I didn't lie," he said. "You knew who I was when you picked me up."

We hear the story and shake our heads. He should have known better, we bemoan. And we are right. He should have. And so should we. But don't we do the same? Don't we believe the lies of the snake? Don't we pick up what we should leave alone?

The Christians in Corinth did. One snake after another had hissed lies in their ears, and they had believed it. How many lies did they believe? How much time do you have?

The list is long and ugly: sectarianism, disunity, sexual immorality. And that is only the first six chapters. But the book of 1 Corinthians is more than a list of sins; it is an epistle of patience. Paul initiates the letter by calling these Christians "brothers and sisters." He could have called them "heretics" or "hypocrites" or "skirt-chasers," and in so many words he does, but not before he calls them brothers and sisters.

He patiently teaches them about worship, unity, the role of women, and the Lord's Supper. He writes as if he can see them face to face. He is disturbed but not despondent. Angry but not desperate. His driving passion is love. And his treatise on love in chapter 13 remains the greatest essay ever penned.

The letter, however personal, is not just for Corinth. It is for all who have heard the whisper and felt the fangs. We, like the man in the story, should have known better. We, like the Corinthians, sometimes need a second chance.

AUTHOR AND DATE

Paul, who persecuted the early church before his life was radically altered by meeting the risen Jesus on the road to Damascus (see Acts 9:1–31). Paul first arrived in Corinth after a disappointing visit to Athens, where he was unable to establish a church (see 17:16–34). There he met two Jewish believers and fellow tentmakers, Priscilla and Aquila, and together they formed a church. Paul's success in Corinth led to both Jews and Gentiles, from all backgrounds and walks of life, accepting Christ and joining the community. In turn, this would lead to certain challenges among the believers as they sought to separate from their past and walk in their new lives in Christ, which Paul would address in a series of letters. It is likely Paul wrote 1 Corinthians

c. AD 55 from Ephesus and sent Titus, his fellow minister, to deliver it. Sosthenes, whom Paul mentions in the opening of the letter, could have been the scribe.

SITUATION

After spending some time in Antioch, Paul set out on what has become known as his "third missionary journey." This time he travelled alone and visited many of the churches he had established during his first missionary journey and settled in the city of Ephesus (see Acts 18:23–24). While there, he began to receive reports about what was happening in the church in Corinth that he had previously founded. The believers were rejecting his instructions to stay away from sexual immorality (see 1 Corinthians 5:9), were engaging in other immoral practices (see 5:1–2; 6:12–20), were struggling with divisions (see 1:10–12), and were having legal disputes (see 6:1–11). The believers also had questions about marriage (see 7:1–40), eating food sacrificed to idols (see 8:1-13), spiritual gifts (see 12:1–31), and the resurrection (see 15:12–58). Paul sought to cover each of these issues—and more—in his letter.

KEY THEMES

- The church, as the body of Christ, should be unified in the same way a physical body is united.
- God calls His people to sexual purity.
- We must honor God within our human relationships.
- Love is the greatest of all gifts.

KEY VERSE

If I speak in the tongues of men or of angels, but do not have love, I am only a resounding gong or a clanging cymbal (1 Corinthians 13:1).

CONTENTS

I. Divisions Among the Church (1:1–4:21)

II. Sexual Purity (5:1–6:20)

III. Answers to Questions (7:1–14:40)

IV. Jesus' Resurrection and Paul's Closing (15:1–16:24)

THE FOLLY OF HUMAN WISDOM

The message of the cross is foolishness to
those who are perishing, but to us who are
being saved it is the power of God.
1 CORINTHIANS 1:18 NKJV

REFLECTION

Some things don't change. Today, as in Paul's day, believing in Jesus is a stumbling block for some people. They label the gospel message as too simple, too unbelievable, or too unrealistic. Which aspects of the gospel—such as Jesus' life, death, and resurrection—do you think are difficult for the modern mind to understand and accept? Why?

SITUATION

The apostle Paul begins this first of several letters to the church in Corinth with compliments and concerns. He has heard about their amazing potential but also their disheartening divisions. The church is a house divided, and Paul knows they will not stand if they remain that way. He pleads for their unity, emphasizing that all who have received the message of the gospel—regardless of their status, position, or how wise they seem in the world's eyes—are one in Christ. Paul reminds the believers that this status they have received is a gift from God.

OBSERVATION

Read 1 Corinthians 1:18–31 from the New International Version or the New King James Version

New International Version

[18] For the message of the cross is foolishness to those who are perishing, but to us who are being saved it is the power of God. [19] For it is written:

> "I will destroy the wisdom of the wise;
> the intelligence of the intelligent I will frustrate."

[20] Where is the wise person? Where is the teacher of the law? Where is the philosopher of this age? Has not God made foolish the wisdom of the world? [21] For since in the wisdom of God the world through its wisdom did not know him, God was pleased through the foolishness of what was preached to save those who believe. [22] Jews demand signs and Greeks look for wisdom, [23] but we preach Christ crucified: a stumbling block to Jews and foolishness to Gentiles, [24] but to those whom God has called, both Jews and Greeks, Christ the power of God and the wisdom of God. [25] For the foolishness of God is wiser than human wisdom, and the weakness of God is stronger than human strength.

[26] Brothers and sisters, think of what you were when you were called. Not many of you were wise by human standards; not many were influential; not many were of noble birth. [27] But God chose the foolish things of the world to shame the wise; God chose the weak things of the world to shame the strong. [28] God chose the lowly things of this world and the despised things—and the things that are not—to nullify the things that are, [29] so that no one may boast before him. [30] It is because of him that you are in Christ Jesus, who has become for us wisdom from God—that is, our righteousness, holiness and redemption. [31] Therefore, as it is written: "Let the one who boasts boast in the Lord."

NEW KING JAMES VERSION

[18] For the message of the cross is foolishness to those who are perishing, but to us who are being saved it is the power of God. [19] For it is written:

> "I will destroy the wisdom of the wise,
> And bring to nothing the understanding of the prudent."

[20] Where is the wise? Where is the scribe? Where is the disputer of this age? Has not God made foolish the wisdom of this world? [21] For since,

in the wisdom of God, the world through wisdom did not know God, it pleased God through the foolishness of the message preached to save those who believe. [22] For Jews request a sign, and Greeks seek after wisdom; [23] but we preach Christ crucified, to the Jews a stumbling block and to the Greeks foolishness, [24] but to those who are called, both Jews and Greeks, Christ the power of God and the wisdom of God. [25] Because the foolishness of God is wiser than men, and the weakness of God is stronger than men.

[26] For you see your calling, brethren, that not many wise according to the flesh, not many mighty, not many noble, are called. [27] But God has chosen the foolish things of the world to put to shame the wise, and God has chosen the weak things of the world to put to shame the things which are mighty; [28] and the base things of the world and the things which are despised God has chosen, and the things which are not, to bring to nothing the things that are, [29] that no flesh should glory in His presence. [30] But of Him you are in Christ Jesus, who became for us wisdom from God—and righteousness and sanctification and redemption— [31] that, as it is written, "He who glories, let him glory in the LORD."

EXPLORATION

1. In what ways can the gospel seem "foolish" to people? Have there been times in your life when all or part of the gospel seemed foolish to you? How?

_____

_____

_____

_____

2. How do Jesus' life and death reveal the wisdom and power of God?

_____

_____

_____

3. In what ways is God's wisdom different from the world's wisdom?

4. What does Paul ask the Corinthian believers to remember in verse 26? Why do you think Paul feels the need to point this out to them?

5. What does Paul mean when he says that God "chose the foolish things of the world to shame the wise" (verse 27)?

6. So, what do believers have to brag about? There's certainly a difference between talking about something or someone praiseworthy and talking about yourself. There are different types of bragging. To which do you think Paul is referring?

INSPIRATION

Is there really a God? Can we know he truly exists? Can we know he's not just a product of our imagination?

The wisdom of the world tells us there is no answer to these questions. It says we can only know what is real by what we can verify through our five senses. It instructs us that belief in God is the same as believing in myths and fairy tales. To the world, trusting in God and following in his ways is utter foolishness.

To this attitude, the apostle Paul replies, "The message of the cross is foolishness to those who are perishing, but to us who are being saved it is the power of God. For it is written: 'I will destroy the wisdom of the wise, and bring to nothing the understanding of the prudent'" (1 Corinthians 1:18–19 NKJV).

Belief in God is not *blind* faith. Belief means having a firm conviction ("I believe this to be true"), not merely hoping it's true ("I believe the Cubs will win the World Series"). It's the kind of assurance you get standing on a huge rock. So how can people get to that place in their belief in God?

Space: Look to the skies. Two hundred billion stars just in the Milky Way galaxy. Billions of galaxies and expanding. Where does it end? How did it all begin?

Earth: Look to creation. So many varieties. So much beauty. A circle of life. How did it all come to be? Why does it work in perfect synchronicity?

Ethics: Look to our morals. A common sense of right and wrong shared by people in different countries and different times in history. Murder is always bad. Courage is always good. Who programmed us?

Bible: Look to God's Word. Examine the wisdom. Experience the stories. Trace its preservation throughout time. How did it remain so well intact despite wars and opposition?

Empty tomb: Look to the resurrection. So many of those who claimed to have seen the risen Lord died with that testimony on their lips. Would they die for a lie? Or did they believe they, too, would rise?

Jesus: Look to him. No other man in history has caused so many questions, stirred so many hearts, given so many answers. Could he be who he said he was?

God is not a product of our imagination. He's far more than any of us could imagine, and he is truth. (Adapted from *Max on Life* by Max Lucado.)

REACTION

7. In what ways has the world tried to convince you that believing in God is foolish?

_____

_____

_____

_____

_____

8. In what situations have you sought God's guidance rather than relying on your intellect or the advice of others? Explain the circumstances and the outcome.

_____

_____

_____

_____

_____

9. How can you better ignore the false messages around you and think more like God?

_____

_____

_____

_____

10. Why is it important to recognize the limits of human wisdom?

_____

_____

_____

_____

11. In what ways can you determine if an idea or plan is based on worldly thinking or biblical teaching?

_____

_____

_____

_____

_____

_____

12. What are some benefits of living according to God's wisdom instead of human wisdom?

_____

_____

_____

_____

_____

LIFE LESSONS

Two dangers immediately head the list when it comes to human wisdom: (1) it sometimes works, and (2) it's mixed with true wisdom. Human wisdom can seem effective and, for a while, those who follow it may achieve success. Human wisdom declares, "It's only wrong if you get caught," and there will be those who do wrong who will appear to get away with it. At the same time, human wisdom is mixed. Elements of human wisdom are often borrowed from God's wisdom—but the conclusions and applications are wrong. For this reason, we must always put human wisdom through truth grid, a test, by comparing it to the wisdom we find in the Bible. In fact, one of the priceless roles of God's Word is the way it tests and corrects human wisdom.

DEVOTION

Father, too often the lies of the world drown out your voice. Give us ears to hear you and hearts willing to obey. Help us to stand against the pressure to seek success and power. Give us the strength to choose the timeless truths of your Word over the fleeting promises of the world. And Father, confirm only those thoughts and plans that conform to your will.

JOURNALING

In light of Paul's words in 1 Corinthians 1:18–31, how can you make better decisions?

FOR FURTHER READING

To complete the book of 1 Corinthians during this twelve-part study, read 1 Corinthians 1:1–31. For more Bible passages on the limits of human wisdom, read Proverbs 3:5–7; Ecclesiastes 1:12–18; Jeremiah 9:23–24; Ezekiel 28:2–7; Matthew 11:25; and 1 Corinthians 3:19–20.

GOD'S WISDOM REVEALED

*"What no eye has seen, what no ear has heard, and
what no human mind has conceived"—the things
God has prepared for those who love him—these are
the things God has revealed to us by his Spirit.*

1 CORINTHIANS 2:9–10

REFLECTION

In the last lesson, we saw that we need to have discernment and not just follow the world's wisdom. What are your "tests" for discerning good advice? Think of someone who consistently gives you good advice. How has that person's wise counsel helped you in a specific situation?

SITUATION

The Corinthians were not only divided but also argumentative. Although the believers in Corinth came from humble backgrounds, some of them seemed eager to claim worldly wisdom rather than standing together with Christ. In response, Paul reminded them of his own behavior among them. He reiterated that his impact was not based on charismatic debates but on a simple message of Christ. He called them back to their original point of faith.

OBSERVATION

Read 1 Corinthians 2:6–16 from the New International Version or the New King James Version.

NEW INTERNATIONAL VERSION
[6] We do, however, speak a message of wisdom among the mature, but not the wisdom of this age or of the rulers of this age, who are coming to nothing. [7] No, we declare God's wisdom, a mystery that has been hidden and that God destined for our glory before time began. [8] None

of the rulers of this age understood it, for if they had, they would not have crucified the Lord of glory. [9] However, as it is written:

> "What no eye has seen,
>   what no ear has heard,
>   and what no human mind has conceived"—
>   the things God has prepared for those who love him—

[10] these are the things God has revealed to us by his Spirit.

The Spirit searches all things, even the deep things of God. [11] For who knows a person's thoughts except their own spirit within them? In the same way no one knows the thoughts of God except the Spirit of God. [12] What we have received is not the spirit of the world, but the Spirit who is from God, so that we may understand what God has freely given us. [13] This is what we speak, not in words taught us by human wisdom but in words taught by the Spirit, explaining spiritual realities with Spirit-taught words. [14] The person without the Spirit does not accept the things that come from the Spirit of God but considers them foolishness, and cannot understand them because they are discerned only through the Spirit. [15] The person with the Spirit makes judgments about all things, but such a person is not subject to merely human judgments, [16] for,

> "Who has known the mind of the Lord
>   so as to instruct him?"

But we have the mind of Christ.

NEW KING JAMES VERSION

[6] However, we speak wisdom among those who are mature, yet not the wisdom of this age, nor of the rulers of this age, who are coming to nothing. [7] But we speak the wisdom of God in a mystery, the hidden wisdom which God ordained before the ages for our glory, [8] which

none of the rulers of this age knew; for had they known, they would not have crucified the Lord of glory.

⁹ But as it is written:

> "Eye has not seen, nor ear heard,
> Nor have entered into the heart of man
> The things which God has prepared for those who love Him."

¹⁰ But God has revealed them to us through His Spirit. For the Spirit searches all things, yes, the deep things of God. ¹¹ For what man knows the things of a man except the spirit of the man which is in him? Even so no one knows the things of God except the Spirit of God. ¹² Now we have received, not the spirit of the world, but the Spirit who is from God, that we might know the things that have been freely given to us by God.

¹³ These things we also speak, not in words which man's wisdom teaches but which the Holy Spirit teaches, comparing spiritual things with spiritual. ¹⁴ But the natural man does not receive the things of the Spirit of God, for they are foolishness to him; nor can he know them, because they are spiritually discerned. ¹⁵ But he who is spiritual judges all things, yet he himself is rightly judged by no one. ¹⁶ For "who has known the mind of the Lord that he may instruct Him?" But we have the mind of Christ.

EXPLORATION

1. Why do you think God keep some things hidden from you? How might knowing a lot more turn into danger for you?

_____

_____

_____

_____

_____

_____

2. What does Paul mean when he says that if the "rulers of this age" had understood God's wisdom, they would not have crucified Christ?

_____

_____

_____

_____

3. In what ways can you know God's thoughts and plans?

_____

_____

_____

_____

4. What are some of the ways the Holy Spirit helps believers (see John 14:26 and 16:13–15)?

_____

_____

_____

_____

5. How does Paul explain in this passage why a person without the Holy Spirit is unable to understand spiritual truths?

_____

_____

_____

_____

6. What does it mean to "have the mind of Christ" (see Romans 11:34 and Philippians 2:5)?

_____

_____

_____

_____

INSPIRATION

Does God have an ego problem?

No, but we do. We are about as responsible with applause as I was with the cake I won in the first grade. In the grand finale of the musical chairs competition, guess who had a seat? And guess what the little red headed, freckle-faced boy won? A tender, moist, coconut cake. And guess what the boy wanted to do that night in one sitting? Eat the whole thing! Not half of it. Not a piece of it. All of it! After all, I'd won it.

But you know what my folks did? They rationed the cake. They gave me only what I could handle. Knowing that today's binge is tomorrow's bellyache, they made sure I didn't get sick on my success.

God does the same. He takes the cake. He takes the credit, not because he needs it, but because he knows we can't handle it. We aren't content with a bite of adulation; we tend to swallow it all. It messes with our systems. The praise swells our heads and shrinks our brains, and pretty soon we start thinking we had something to do with our survival. Pretty soon we forget we were made out of dirt and rescued from sin.

Pretty soon we start praying like the fellow at the religious caucus: "God, I thank you that the world has people like me. The man on the corner needs welfare—I don't. The prostitute on the street has AIDS—I don't. The drunk at the bar needs alcohol—I don't. The gay caucus needs morality—I don't. I thank you that the world has people like me."

Fortunately, there was a man in the same meeting who had deflected all the applause. Too contrite even to look to the skies, he bowed and prayed, "God, have mercy on me, a sinner. Like my brother on welfare, I'm dependent on grace. Like my sister with AIDS, I'm infected with mistakes. Like my friend who drinks, I need something to ease my pain. And as you love and give direction to the gay, grant some to me as well. Have mercy on me, a sinner."

After telling a story like that, Jesus said, "I tell you that this man, rather than the other, went home justified before God. For all those who exalt themselves will be humbled, and those who humble themselves will be exalted" (Luke 18:14). (From *Traveling Light* by Max Lucado.)

REACTION

7. In what ways do people try to gain wisdom? Why do they want it?

8. What happens when you rely on human wisdom instead of God's wisdom?

9. When has the Holy Spirit helped you understand or apply God's Word?

10. What practical steps can you take to reduce the risk of making foolish decisions?

11. What sometimes keeps you from seeking God's help?

_____

_____

_____

_____

12. In what ways can you depend more on God's Spirit to help you make wise decisions?

_____

_____

_____

_____

LIFE LESSONS

The most difficult part of God's wisdom is that it usually requires us to do what we don't want to do and asks us not to do what we want to do. God's wisdom offends our wills more than our minds. Partly because of its eternal source, God's wisdom acts with a larger perspective in mind. And God's wisdom is always trustworthy. Just as I discovered my parents' wisdom in rationing out my cake, so God's will wisely give us what we need and what is best.

DEVOTION

Father, your plans for us are perfect. Yet we often doubt your promises and assume we can take better care of ourselves than our Creator. Forgive us for ignoring the truth in your Word. Tune our ears to your Spirit's voice and teach us to follow your ways. May our lives testify to your great wisdom and power.

JOURNALING

In what situation today do you need God's wisdom?

FOR FURTHER READING

To complete the book of 1 Corinthians during this twelve-part study, read 1 Corinthians 2:1–16. For more Bible passages on God's wisdom, read Psalm 111:10; Proverbs 2:6; Isaiah 11:2; Jeremiah 10:12; Ephesians 1:16–17; Colossians 2:3; 2 Timothy 3:15; and James 1:5.

LESSON THREE

WORK THAT LASTS

So then neither he who plants is anything, nor he who waters, but God who gives the increase.
1 CORINTHIANS 3:7 NKJV

REFLECTION

There are countless ways to spend one's time. But think about how your life is enriched by those who choose to give of their time in a way that benefits you. What are some of the desires and drives that motivate people to volunteer in the community or your church?

_____

_____

_____

_____

SITUATION

The Corinthian church was a divided congregation, and part of the divisiveness was the result of the believers forming "fan clubs" for certain spiritual leaders. Some of the people followed a learned teacher named Apollos, a native of Alexandria who had been instructed in the gospel by Priscilla and Aquila (see Acts 18:24–28). Others had loyalty only to Paul or to Peter. This appalled the apostle. They were missing the point entirely. Their allegiance needed to be firmly rooted in one place—in Christ alone. To address this problem, Paul pointed out in this next section of his letter the uselessness of any work done without that foundation.

OBSERVATION

Read 1 Corinthians 3:3–15 from the New International Version or the New King James Version.

New International Version

³ You are still worldly. For since there is jealousy and quarreling among you, are you not worldly? Are you not acting like mere humans? ⁴ For

when one says, "I follow Paul," and another, "I follow Apollos," are you not mere human beings?

⁵ What, after all, is Apollos? And what is Paul? Only servants, through whom you came to believe—as the Lord has assigned to each his task. ⁶ I planted the seed, Apollos watered it, but God has been making it grow. ⁷ So neither the one who plants nor the one who waters is anything, but only God, who makes things grow. ⁸ The one who plants and the one who waters have one purpose, and they will each be rewarded according to their own labor. ⁹ For we are co-workers in God's service; you are God's field, God's building.

¹⁰ By the grace God has given me, I laid a foundation as a wise builder, and someone else is building on it. But each one should build with care. ¹¹ For no one can lay any foundation other than the one already laid, which is Jesus Christ. ¹² If anyone builds on this foundation using gold, silver, costly stones, wood, hay or straw, ¹³ their work will be shown for what it is, because the Day will bring it to light. It will be revealed with fire, and the fire will test the quality of each person's work. ¹⁴ If what has been built survives, the builder will receive a reward. ¹⁵ If it is burned up, the builder will suffer loss but yet will be saved—even though only as one escaping through the flames.

NEW KING JAMES VERSION

³ For you are still carnal. For where there are envy, strife, and divisions among you, are you not carnal and behaving like mere men? ⁴ For when one says, "I am of Paul," and another, "I am of Apollos," are you not carnal?

⁵ Who then is Paul, and who is Apollos, but ministers through whom you believed, as the Lord gave to each one? ⁶ I planted, Apollos watered, but God gave the increase. ⁷ So then neither he who plants is anything, nor he who waters, but God who gives the increase. ⁸ Now he who plants and he who waters are one, and each one will receive his own reward according to his own labor.

⁹ For we are God's fellow workers; you are God's field, you are God's building. ¹⁰ According to the grace of God which was given to me, as a

wise master builder I have laid the foundation, and another builds on it. But let each one take heed how he builds on it. [11] For no other foundation can anyone lay than that which is laid, which is Jesus Christ. [12] Now if anyone builds on this foundation with gold, silver, precious stones, wood, hay, straw, [13] each one's work will become clear; for the Day will declare it, because it will be revealed by fire; and the fire will test each one's work, of what sort it is. [14] If anyone's work which he has built on it endures, he will receive a reward. [15] If anyone's work is burned, he will suffer loss; but he himself will be saved, yet so as through fire.

EXPLORATION

1. How does Paul describe his and Apollos' role in the Corinthian church?

_____

_____

_____

_____

2. Paul makes it clear to the believers in Corinth that Jesus is the foundation of the church. What does that mean in today's world?

_____

_____

_____

_____

3. In what authentic and lasting ways can you build on the foundation that God has laid?

_____

_____

_____

_____

4. Paul states that God will test the quality of your work as fire tests the quality of building materials (see verse 13). What kinds of work will withstand that test?

_____

_____

_____

_____

5. What are the rewards of building God's kingdom faithfully and with the best materials?

_____

_____

_____

6. Paul compares work for God that is less than excellent to a straw house that will burn up in the fire of judgment. What kind of behavior or service is like a straw house?

_____

_____

_____

_____

INSPIRATION

A large American food company released the perfect cake mix. It required no additives. No eggs, no sugar. Just mix some water with the powder, pop the pan in the oven, and presto! Prepare yourself for a treat.

One problem surfaced. No one purchased the product! Puzzled, the manufacturer conducted surveys, identified the reason, and reissued the cake with a slight alteration. The instructions now called for the cook to add one egg. Sales skyrocketed!

Why are we like that? What makes us want to add to what is already complete? Paul asked the same questions. People puzzled him by adding their work to a finished project. Not eggs to a recipe but requirements for salvation. Not much, just one small rule—like a person must be circumcised to be saved.

Such talk rankled the apostle. He declared, "It isn't the cutting of our bodies that makes us children of God; it is worshiping him with our spirits. . . . God's way of making us right with himself depends on faith—counting on *Christ alone*" (Philippians 3:3, 9 TLB, emphasis mine). Paul proclaimed a pure grace: no mixtures, no additives, no alterations. The work of Christ is the bungee cord for the soul. Trust it and take the plunge.

We quickly side with Paul on the circumcision controversy. The whole discussion sounds odd to our Western ears. But is it so strange? We may not teach Jesus + circumcision, but how about:

Jesus + evangelism: *How many people have you led to Christ this year?* Or: Jesus + contributions: *Are you giving all you can to the church?* Or:

Jesus + mysticism: *You do offer penance and pray to the Virgin Mary, don't you?* Or: Jesus + heritage: *Were you raised in "the church"?* Or:

Jesus + doctrine: *When you were baptized, was the water running or still? Deep or shallow? Hot or cold?*

Legalism. The theology of "Jesus + . . ." Legalists don't dismiss Christ. They trust in Christ a lot. But they don't trust in Christ alone. (From *It's Not About Me* by Max Lucado.)

REACTION

7. What should be the driving force behind your work for God?

_____

_____

_____

_____

_____

8. Why is it tempting to evaluate your success based on external results? What happens when you give in to that temptation?

_____

_____

_____

_____

_____

_____

9. According to Paul, what kind of work counts for eternity?

_____

_____

_____

_____

_____

_____

10. What obstacles tend to keep you from getting more involved in ministry?

_____

_____

_____

_____

_____

_____

11. In what ways can you evaluate the quality of your service?

_____

_____

_____

_____

_____

_____

12. What are some practical ways you can invest yourself more in God's kingdom?

_____

_____

_____

_____

_____

_____

_____

_____

_____

LIFE LESSONS

Healthy Christian mentor relationships can easily take a wrong turn. We need to learn from believers who are more experienced than we are, but we make a mistake if our faith begins to rest more on our teacher than on Christ. Trustworthy leaders always point to Jesus, not to themselves. They expect us to follow them only so long as they are clearly following Christ. The work we do for Christ must never be seen as an added part of the foundation that rests on Jesus alone. Gold flows from gratitude-based actions toward Christ. Any other motivation tends to produce wood, hay, and stubble.

DEVOTION

Father, thank you for laying the perfect foundation for your church. Now show us how to build on that foundation. Give us a burning desire to build your church. Help us to see what is important and what is lasting. Let us make decisions based on eternity and not on temporary possessions. Most of all, Father, help us to seek your kingdom and your righteousness.

JOURNALING

What is your specific role in building God's church?

FOR FURTHER READING

To complete the book of 1 Corinthians during this twelve-part study, read 1 Corinthians 3:1–23. For more Bible passages on work that lasts, read Luke 12:33; John 6:27; 2 Corinthians 4:17–18; Colossians 3:23–24; and Hebrews 10:34–35.

LESSON FOUR

SERVING CHRIST

We work hard with our own hands. When we are cursed, we bless; when we are persecuted, we endure it; when we are slandered, we answer kindly.

1 CORINTHIANS 4:12–13

REFLECTION

Think of someone who has served Christ for many years—whether that person is a popular figure in culture or known to you personally. What are some ways that person's example has inspired you? Ware are some of the traits in that person that you want to develop in your life?

_____

_____

_____

_____

SITUATION

Groups within the Corinthian church were not only aligning themselves with the names of leaders such as Paul and Apollos, but they were also developing an attitude of independence and pride among themselves. They were using recognizable names but practicing their own brand of spirituality. Paul had to confront their selective and comfortable spiritual lives in this next portion of his letter and talk about the nature of true followers of Christ.

OBSERVATION

Read 1 Corinthians 4:6–19 from the New International Version or the New King James Version.

New International Version

6 Now, brothers and sisters, I have applied these things to myself and Apollos for your benefit, so that you may learn from us the meaning of the saying, "Do not go beyond what is written." Then you will not be puffed up in being a follower of one of us over against the other. 7 For

who makes you different from anyone else? What do you have that you did not receive? And if you did receive it, why do you boast as though you did not?

[8] Already you have all you want! Already you have become rich! You have begun to reign—and that without us! How I wish that you really had begun to reign so that we also might reign with you! [9] For it seems to me that God has put us apostles on display at the end of the procession, like those condemned to die in the arena. We have been made a spectacle to the whole universe, to angels as well as to human beings. [10] We are fools for Christ, but you are so wise in Christ! We are weak, but you are strong! You are honored, we are dishonored! [11] To this very hour we go hungry and thirsty, we are in rags, we are brutally treated, we are homeless. [12] We work hard with our own hands. When we are cursed, we bless; when we are persecuted, we endure it; [13] when we are slandered, we answer kindly. We have become the scum of the earth, the garbage of the world—right up to this moment.

[14] I am writing this not to shame you but to warn you as my dear children. [15] Even if you had ten thousand guardians in Christ, you do not have many fathers, for in Christ Jesus I became your father through the gospel. [16] Therefore I urge you to imitate me. [17] For this reason I have sent to you Timothy, my son whom I love, who is faithful in the Lord. He will remind you of my way of life in Christ Jesus, which agrees with what I teach everywhere in every church.

[18] Some of you have become arrogant, as if I were not coming to you. [19] But I will come to you very soon, if the Lord is willing, and then I will find out not only how these arrogant people are talking, but what power they have.

NEW KING JAMES VERSION

[6] Now these things, brethren, I have figuratively transferred to myself and Apollos for your sakes, that you may learn in us not to think beyond what is written, that none of you may be puffed up on behalf of one against the other. [7] For who makes you differ from another?

And what do you have that you did not receive? Now if you did indeed receive it, why do you boast as if you had not received it?

⁸ You are already full! You are already rich! You have reigned as kings without us—and indeed I could wish you did reign, that we also might reign with you! ⁹ For I think that God has displayed us, the apostles, last, as men condemned to death; for we have been made a spectacle to the world, both to angels and to men. ¹⁰ We are fools for Christ's sake, but you are wise in Christ! We are weak, but you are strong! You are distinguished, but we are dishonored! ¹¹ To the present hour we both hunger and thirst, and we are poorly clothed, and beaten, and homeless. ¹² And we labor, working with our own hands. Being reviled, we bless; being persecuted, we endure; ¹³ being defamed, we entreat. We have been made as the filth of the world, the off scouring of all things until now.

¹⁴ I do not write these things to shame you, but as my beloved children I warn you. ¹⁵ For though you might have ten thousand instructors in Christ, yet you do not have many fathers; for in Christ Jesus I have begotten you through the gospel. ¹⁶ Therefore I urge you, imitate me. ¹⁷ For this reason I have sent Timothy to you, who is my beloved and faithful son in the Lord, who will remind you of my ways in Christ, as I teach everywhere in every church.

¹⁸ Now some are puffed up, as though I were not coming to you. ¹⁹ But I will come to you shortly, if the Lord wills, and I will know, not the word of those who are puffed up, but the power.

EXPLORATION

1. Paul saw evidence of *spiritual pride* in the early church—of one Christian judging whether a fellow believer was a "good" follower of Jesus. Why do you think this troubled him?

_____

_____

_____

_____

2. Your abilities and talents are gifts from God. As you identify them and begin to use them, what should keep you from thinking that you are better than others?

_____

_____

_____

_____

3. Is there anything wrong with taking the credit for your accomplishments? Why or why not?

_____

_____

_____

_____

4. Paul believed apostles should stand in last place. What does that tell you about Paul's attitude toward status and position (particularly compared to how people weigh status and position today)?

_____

_____

_____

5. In what way did Paul encourage the Corinthian believers to imitate him?

_____

_____

_____

6. What should you be willing to give up to serve Christ?

_____

_____

_____

_____

INSPIRATION

The scene is almost spooky: a tall, unfinished tower looming solitarily on a dusty plain. Its base is wide and strong but covered with weeds. Large stones originally intended for use in the tower lie forsaken on the ground. Buckets, hammers, and pulleys—all lie abandoned. The silhouette cast by the structure is lean and lonely.

Not too long ago, this tower was buzzing with activity. A bystander would have been impressed with the smooth-running construction of the world's first skyscraper. One group of workers stirred freshly made mortar. Another team pulled bricks out of the oven. A third group carried the bricks to the construction site while a fourth shouldered the load up a winding path to the top of the tower where it was firmly set in place.

Their dream was a tower. A tower that would be taller than anyone had ever dreamed. A tower that would punch through the clouds and scratch the heavens. And what was the purpose of the tower? To glorify God? No. To try to find God? No. To call people to look upward to God? Try again. To provide a heavenly haven of prayer? Still wrong.

The purpose of the work caused its eventual abortion. The method was right. The plan was effective. But the motive was wrong. Dead wrong. Read these minutes from the Tower Planning Committee Meeting and see what I mean: "Come, let us build ourselves a city, with a tower that reaches to the heavens, so that [watch out] we may make a name for ourselves" (Genesis 11:4).

Why was the tower being built? Selfishness. Pure, 100-percent selfishness. The bricks were made of inflated egos and the mortar was made of pride. Men were giving sweat and blood for a pillar. Why? So that somebody's name could be remembered.

We have a name for that: *blind ambition*. We make heroes out of people who are ambitious. And rightly so. This world would be in sad shape without people who dream of touching the heavens. Ambition is that grit in the soul which creates disenchantment with the ordinary and puts the dare into dreams.

But left unchecked, it becomes an insatiable addition to power and prestige—a roaring hunger for achievement that devours people as a lion devours an animal, leaving behind only the skeletal remains of relationships.

Blind ambition. Distorted values. God won't tolerate it. He didn't then, and he won't now. He took the "Climb to Heaven Campaign" into his hands. With one sweep, he painted the tower gray with confusion and sent workers babbling in all directions. He took man's greatest achievement and blew it into the winds like a child blows a dandelion.

Are you building any towers? Examine your motives. And remember the statement imprinted on the base of the windswept Tower of Babel: blind ambition is a giant step away from God and one step closer to catastrophe. (From *God Came Near* by Max Lucado.)

REACTION

7. What is the potential danger in trying to achieve great things for God?

---

8. What are some ways selfish ambition can create problems in the church?

---

9. How can you determine whether your service to God is Christ-centered or self-centered? What examples would you use to illustrate this principle?

---

10. In what ways can you curb your appetite for prestige and power? What do you have to watch for in your relational and spiritual "diet"?

_____

_____

_____

11. When God gives you success in various endeavors, how can you guard against pride?

_____

_____

_____

12. How can you give God appropriate credit for the things he has accomplished through you?

_____

_____

_____

LIFE LESSONS

Refusing to take credit for our part in something good doesn't necessarily indicate a lack of pride. And taking credit for our contribution doesn't necessarily indicate pride. Paul admitted that he was the "father" of the Corinthian church. That wasn't pride; it was a statement of fact used to anchor a significant lesson. Paul's counsel to the Roman believers should be our constant guide: "For I say, through the grace given to me, to everyone who is among you, not to think of himself more highly than he ought to think, but to think soberly, as God has dealt to each one a measure of faith" (Romans 12:3 NKJV). Spiritual pride is a persistent pit that lies alongside a believer's pathway. We are in greatest danger of stumbling into that void in the moments after we think we have just done something humble.

DEVOTION

O Father, forgive us for our arrogance, for acting as though we can accomplish great things on our own. We are nothing without you. Teach us to recognize our complete dependence on you and to surrender our desires and ambitions. Make our service more pleasing in your sight.

JOURNALING

What personal goals or desires do you need to reevaluate today?

FOR FURTHER READING

To complete the book of 1 Corinthians during this twelve-part study, read 1 Corinthians 4:1–6:20. For more Bible passages on serving Christ, read Matthew 20:25–28; John 12:25–26; Romans 12:10–11; 14:17–18; and Ephesians 6:7.

LESSON FIVE

SELF-SACRIFICE

*For though I am free from all men, I have made
myself a servant to all, that I might win the
more. . . . I have become all things to all men,
that I might by all means save some.*

1 CORINTHIANS 9:19, 22 NKJV

REFLECTION

Of all the creatures on the earth, human beings are among the least self-sufficient. We arrive naked and desperately in need of covering that someone else must provide. In the same way, the sacrifices of others are necessary in encouraging our spiritual growth after we choose to follow Christ. When was a time that someone sacrificed his or her own needs to help you?

SITUATION

In the next parts of Paul's letter, he deals with specific issues in the Corinthian church, including incest among believers, lawsuits, and sexual immorality. He also answers the believers' questions on matters such as marriage, singleness, and food sacrificed to idols. Paul now turns to addressing issues of divisiveness and self-centeredness in the church that—although posing as Christian freedom—has created chaos in the lives of the community. In this next section of his letter, he warns believers that an overemphasis on freedom, rather than on Christ, can quickly lead to bondage. Freedom must be balanced with self-sacrifice for Christ's sake.

OBSERVATION

*Read 1 Corinthians 9:16–22 from the New International
Version or the New King James Version*

NEW INTERNATIONAL VERSION

[16] For when I preach the gospel, I cannot boast, since I am compelled to preach. Woe to me if I do not preach the gospel! [17] If I preach voluntarily, I have a reward; if not voluntarily, I am simply discharging the trust committed to me. [18] What then is my reward? Just this: that in preaching the gospel I may offer it free of charge, and so not make full use of my rights as a preacher of the gospel.

[19] Though I am free and belong to no one, I have made myself a slave to everyone, to win as many as possible. [20] To the Jews I became like a Jew, to win the Jews. To those under the law I became like one under the law (though I myself am not under the law), so as to win those under the law. [21] To those not having the law I became like one not having the law (though I am not free from God's law but am under Christ's law), so as to win those not having the law. [22] To the weak I became weak, to win the weak. I have become all things to all people so that by all possible means I might save some.

NEW KING JAMES VERSION

[16] For if I preach the gospel, I have nothing to boast of, for necessity is laid upon me; yes, woe is me if I do not preach the gospel! [17] For if I do this willingly, I have a reward; but if against my will, I have been entrusted with a stewardship. [18] What is my reward then? That when I preach the gospel, I may present the gospel of Christ without charge, that I may not abuse my authority in the gospel.

[19] For though I am free from all men, I have made myself a servant to all, that I might win the more; [20] and to the Jews I became as a Jew, that I might win Jews; to those who are under the law, as under the law, that I might win those who are under the law; [21] to those who are without law,

as without law (not being without law toward God, but under law toward Christ), that I might win those who are without law; [22] to the weak I became as weak, that I might win the weak. I have become all things to all men, that I might by all means save some.

EXPLORATION

1. What are some of the reasons Paul provides for why he preaches the gospel? What are his rewards for doing this?

_____

_____

_____

_____

2. Paul notes that he gave up some of his rights to preach the gospel. Why did he do this?

_____

_____

_____

3. What does it mean to become a "slave to everyone" (verse 19)? What kind of language could you use today to get across the same point?

_____

_____

_____

4. Paul was not as concerned with his method of evangelism as with the message he was proclaiming. How can you apply his thinking to the way you share about Jesus today?

_____

_____

_____

5. Think about the times you try to be a witness for Christ. What have you learned in those experiences that you can share with others?

6. What behaviors, attitudes, or beliefs can hinder a person's Christian witness?

INSPIRATION

We are much like Ruthie and Verena Cady. Since their birth in 1984, they have shared much. Just like twins, they have shared a bike, a bed, a room, and toys. They've shared meals and stories and TV shows and birthdays. They shared the same womb before they were born and the same room after they were born. But the bond between Ruthie and Verena goes even further. They share more than toys and treats; they share the same heart.

Their bodies are fused together from the sternum to the waist. Though they have separate nervous systems and distinct personalities, they are sustained by the same, singular three-chambered heart. Neither could survive without the other. Since separation is not an option, cooperation becomes an obligation.

They have learned to work together. Take walking, for example. Their mother assumed they would take turns walking forward or backward. It made sense to her that they would alternate; one facing the front and the other the back. The girls had a better idea. They learned to walk sideways, almost like dancing. And they dance in the same direction . . .

When one has to sit in the corner, so does the other. The innocent party doesn't complain; both learned early that they are stuck together for the good and the bad. Which is just one of the many lessons these girls can teach those of us who live in God's Great House.

Don't we share the same kitchen? Aren't we covered by the same roof and protected by the same walls? We don't sleep in the same bed, but we sleep under the same sky. We aren't sharing one heart . . . but then again maybe we are; for don't we share the same hope for eternity, the same hurt from rejection, and the same hunger to be loved? Like the Cady twins, don't we have the same Father?

We don't pray to *my* Father or ask for *my* daily bread or ask God to forgive *my* sins. In God's house we speak the language of plurality: "*our* Father," "*our* daily bread," "*our* debts," "*our* debtors," "lead *us* not into temptation," and "deliver *us* . . . "

From God's perspective, we have much in common. Jesus lists these common denominators in his prayer. They are easy to find. Every time we see the word *our* or *us*, we find a need. (From *The Great House of God* by Max Lucado.)

REACTION

7. Paul told the Corinthian believers that he gave up his own rights, preferences, and styles in order to share the gospel. How does this contradict human nature?

----

8. Why is it so difficult for believers to give up their rights? What are some of the rights that believers tend struggle over in the church?

9. What are some of the benefits of self-sacrifice (see Matthew 19:21 and Luke 14:26)?

10. How can a spirit of humility contributes to effectively sharing the gospel with others?

11. How can you combat the natural human tendency to fight for your rights when it comes to loving others as God loves them?

12. What are some practical ways that you can better cultivate a spirit of humility?

_____

_____

_____

_____

_____

LIFE LESSONS

Like love, humility has less to do with feelings than it has to do with decisions, motivations, and actions. Humility as a feeling is probably similar to nitroglycerin—shake it and it blows up. But God's Word gives us numerous guidelines and challenges to live humbly. In a world that boldly encourages us to think about ourselves first, the discipline of humility chooses to focus on others. So often our real needs are met as we seek to meet the needs of others. Self-sacrifice doesn't look like fun, feel like fun, or seem like fun. But then fun isn't the final goal, is it? The greatest example of self-sacrifice wasn't carried out because it was fun; it was carried out because of the ultimate joy that would result. "Looking unto Jesus, the author and finisher of our faith, who for the joy that was set before Him endured the cross, despising the shame, and has sat down at the right hand of the throne of God" (Hebrews 12:2 NKJV).

DEVOTION

Father, long before we repented or even acknowledged our need for you, you sent your only Son to die for our sins. What amazing love! O Father, help us to be more like you. Fill us with your love, so that we will gladly sacrifice everything to win more souls for you. Take our eyes off ourselves, our rights and desires. May we extend your hand of grace and mercy to the lost.

JOURNALING

What are you willing to give up today to win more people to Christ?

FOR FURTHER READING

To complete the book of 1 Corinthians during this twelve-part study, read 1 Corinthians 7:1–9:27. For more Bible passages on self-sacrifice, read John 15:13; Romans 12:1–2; Philippians 2:3–5; Hebrews 13:16; and 1 Peter 2:5.

TEMPTATION

*God is faithful; he will not let you be
tempted beyond what you can bear. But
when you are tempted, he will also provide
a way out so that you can endure it.*

1 CORINTHIANS 10:13

REFLECTION

Days without temptation of one kind or another are rare. Having a personal strategy to handle temptation remains a central component to healthy spiritual growth. Think of a time when you felt tempted by something. How did God help you?

_____

_____

_____

_____

_____

_____

SITUATION

Up to this point, Paul has been addressing specific issues he has learned about in the Corinthian church and answering some of the questions they sent to him. But in this next part of his letter, he steps back from this approach to sketch the big picture of God's operations in the world. He begins by pointing out some of the negative events and positive lessons that fill the pages of the Old Testament, and how those lessons can be useful in our lives today.

OBSERVATION

Read 1 Corinthians 10:1–13 from the New International Version or the New King James Version.

NEW INTERNATIONAL VERSION
[1] For I do not want you to be ignorant of the fact, brothers and sisters, that our ancestors were all under the cloud and that they all passed

through the sea. [2] They were all baptized into Moses in the cloud and in the sea. [3] They all ate the same spiritual food [4] and drank the same spiritual drink; for they drank from the spiritual rock that accompanied them, and that rock was Christ. [5] Nevertheless, God was not pleased with most of them; their bodies were scattered in the wilderness.

[6] Now these things occurred as examples to keep us from setting our hearts on evil things as they did. [7] Do not be idolaters, as some of them were; as it is written: "The people sat down to eat and drink and got up to indulge in revelry." [8] We should not commit sexual immorality, as some of them did—and in one day twenty-three thousand of them died. [9] We should not test Christ, as some of them did—and were killed by snakes. [10] And do not grumble, as some of them did—and were killed by the destroying angel.

[11] These things happened to them as examples and were written down as warnings for us, on whom the culmination of the ages has come. [12] So, if you think you are standing firm, be careful that you don't fall! [13] No temptation has overtaken you except what is common to mankind. And God is faithful; he will not let you be tempted beyond what you can bear. But when you are tempted, he will also provide a way out so that you can endure it.

New King James Version

[1] Moreover, brethren, I do not want you to be unaware that all our fathers were under the cloud, all passed through the sea, [2] all were baptized into Moses in the cloud and in the sea, [3] all ate the same spiritual food, [4] and all drank the same spiritual drink. For they drank of that spiritual Rock that followed them, and that Rock was Christ. [5] But with most of them God was not well pleased, for their bodies were scattered in the wilderness.

[6] Now these things became our examples, to the intent that we should not lust after evil things as they also lusted. [7] And do not become idolaters as were some of them. As it is written, "The people sat down to eat and drink, and rose up to play." [8] Nor let us commit sexual immorality,

as some of them did, and in one day twenty-three thousand fell; [9] nor let us tempt Christ, as some of them also tempted, and were destroyed by serpents; [10] nor complain, as some of them also complained, and were destroyed by the destroyer. [11] Now all these things happened to them as examples, and they were written for our admonition, upon whom the ends of the ages have come.

[12] Therefore let him who thinks he stands take heed lest he fall. [13] No temptation has overtaken you except such as is common to man; but God is faithful, who will not allow you to be tempted beyond what you are able, but with the temptation will also make the way of escape, that you may be able to bear it.

EXPLORATION

1. Why do you think Paul begins this section of his letter by reminding the believers in Corinth of the Israelites' history? How would that be relevant to them?

_____

_____

_____

_____

_____

_____

2. What does Paul mean when he says the Israelites were all under the cloud, baptized into Moses, and ate the same spiritual food (see Exodus 13:21–22; 14:21–31; and 16:31–36)?

_____

_____

_____

_____

_____

3. Paul writes that "God was not pleased" with most of the people (verse 5). What are some of the consequences of giving in to temptation again and again (see Numbers 14)?

_____

_____

_____

_____

_____

4. How do the stories in the Bible, like this one Paul tells about the Israelites during the Exodus, serve as examples for how you should lead your life?

_____

_____

_____

_____

5. What does this passage reveal about the difference between your own human nature and God's divine character?

_____

_____

_____

_____

6. What does Paul mean when he warns you should be careful not to fall when you think you are standing firm (see verse 12)? How does overconfidence play into the enemy's hands when it comes to dealing with temptation?

_____

_____

_____

_____

INSPIRATION

Real change is an inside job. You might alter things a day or two with money and systems, but the heart of the matter is, and always will be, the matter of the heart.

Allow me to get specific. Our problem is sin. Not finances. Not budgets. Not overcrowded prisons or drug dealers. Our problem is sin. We are in rebellion against our Creator. We are separated from our Father. We are cut off from the source of life. A new President or policy won't fix that. It can only be solved by God.

That's why the Bible uses drastic terms like *conversion*, *repentance*, and *lost*, and *found*. Society may renovate, but only God re-creates.

Here is a practical exercise to put this truth into practice. The next time alarms go off in your world, ask yourself three questions: *Is there any unconfessed sin in my life? Are there any unresolved conflicts in my world? Are there any unsurrendered worries in my heart?*

Alarms serve a purpose. They signal a problem. Sometimes the problem is out there. More often it's in here. So before you peek outside, take a good look inside. (From *When God Whispers Your Name* by Max Lucado.)

REACTION

7. What are some of the warning signs God uses to help you say no to sin?

_____

_____

_____

_____

_____

_____

_____

8. Why is it easy to overlook or ignore the warning signs that God provides?

9. Think about a time when you gave in to temptation. What might have helped you to be stronger in that instance?

10. Why is it important for you to understand your natural inclination toward sin?

11. How can consistent time in God's Word fortify you in your areas of weakness?

12. What do you plan to do differently the next time you are tempted?

LIFE LESSONS

This passage in 1 Corinthians 10:1–13 represents one of the classic examples of "life lessons" in Scripture. The events in the Bible were recorded for us as examples and admonitions. We can learn from our reading and be warned by the experiences of others. Even when we are confident that we are on track in our spiritual lives, we must "be careful that we don't fall." Our attentiveness can take two forms: first, a continual effort to avoid sin, and second, a willingness to count on God's help when we face temptation.

DEVOTION

Father, your Word says that no temptation will be too strong for us to bear and that you will always show us a way to resist sin. We claim your promises and ask you to give us the strength to use the escape routes you provide. And we pray that in our hours of desperation and weakness, you would help us feel your presence.

JOURNALING

What are some things that keep you from taking the escape routes that God provides?

FOR FURTHER READING

To complete the book of 1 Corinthians during this twelve-part study, read 1 Corinthians 10:1–13. For more Bible passages on temptation, read Matthew 4:1–11; Luke 11:4; Galatians 6:1; 1 Thessalonians 3:5; 1 Timothy 6:9; Hebrews 2:17–18; and James 1:13–15.

LESSON SEVEN

LIBERTY AND LOVE

Therefore, whether you eat or drink, or
whatever you do, do all to the glory of
God. Give no offense, either to the Jews or
to the Greeks or to the church of God.
1 CORINTHIANS 10:31–32 NKJV

REFLECTION

Think for a few moments about what *freedom* means to you. What new freedoms have you enjoyed since you became a Christian? In what ways do you think your freedom in Christ is different from any other freedom you have experienced?

_____

_____

_____

_____

_____

SITUATION

Based on Paul's words in this next section of his letter, it is clear that some of the believers in Corinth were taking their freedom in Christ to extremes. Like the Roman believers, whom Paul addressed in Romans 6, the Corinthian Christians were in danger of using grace as an excuse to sin. Paul needed to show them that if the exercise of spiritual freedom leads to others being misled or harmed, that exercise of freedom has to be re-evaluated. Paul saw numerous instances of this in the Corinthians' lives where this principle could be applied.

OBSERVATION

Read 1 Corinthians 10:23–33 from the New International Version or the New King James Version.

NEW INTERNATIONAL VERSION

23 "I have the right to do anything," you say—but not everything is beneficial. "I have the right to do anything"—but not everything is constructive. 24 No one should seek their own good, but the good of others.

[25] Eat anything sold in the meat market without raising questions of conscience, [26] for, "The earth is the Lord's, and everything in it."

[27] If an unbeliever invites you to a meal and you want to go, eat whatever is put before you without raising questions of conscience. [28] But if someone says to you, "This has been offered in sacrifice," then do not eat it, both for the sake of the one who told you and for the sake of conscience. [29] I am referring to the other person's conscience, not yours. For why is my freedom being judged by another's conscience? [30] If I take part in the meal with thankfulness, why am I denounced because of something I thank God for?

[31] So whether you eat or drink or whatever you do, do it all for the glory of God. [32] Do not cause anyone to stumble, whether Jews, Greeks or the church of God— [33] even as I try to please everyone in every way. For I am not seeking my own good but the good of many, so that they may be saved.

New King James Version

[23] All things are lawful for me, but not all things are helpful; all things are lawful for me, but not all things edify. [24] Let no one seek his own, but each one the other's well-being.

[25] Eat whatever is sold in the meat market, asking no questions for conscience' sake; [26] for "the earth is the LORD's, and all its fullness."

[27] If any of those who do not believe invites you to dinner, and you desire to go, eat whatever is set before you, asking no question for conscience' sake. [28] But if anyone says to you, "This was offered to idols," do not eat it for the sake of the one who told you, and for conscience' sake; for "the earth is the LORD's, and all its fullness." [29] "Conscience," I say, not your own, but that of the other. For why is my liberty judged by another man's conscience? [30] But if I partake with thanks, why am I evil spoken of for the food over which I give thanks?

[31] Therefore, whether you eat or drink, or whatever you do, do all to the glory of God. [32] Give no offense, either to the Jews or to the Greeks or to the church of God, [33] just as I also please all men in all things, not seeking my own profit, but the profit of many, that they may be saved.

EXPLORATION

1. What are some limits that Paul notes need to be placed on a Christian's freedom?

_____

_____

_____

2. What is the relationship between your freedom to enjoy life as a child of God and your limitations to not do certain things out of love for your sisters and brothers in Christ?

_____

_____

_____

3. As a Christian, what should you consider when making ethical decisions?

_____

_____

_____

4. In light of this passage, what does it mean to do "all for the glory of God" (verse 31)?

_____

_____

_____

5. What are some ways you have learned to "walk the line" when it comes to not being bound by other people's legalism but also not doing things that cause other believers to stumble?

_____

_____

_____

6. Based on Paul's advice in this passage, what should always be your primary concern in making lifestyle choices?

_____

_____

_____

INSPIRATION

Life is tough enough as it is. It's even tougher when we're headed in the wrong direction.

One of the incredible abilities of Jesus was to stay on target. His life never got off track. Not once do we find him walking down the wrong side of the fairway. He had no money, no computers, no jets, no administrative assistants or staff, yet Jesus did what many of us fail to do. He kept his life on course.

As Jesus looked across the horizon of his future, he could see many targets. Many flags were flapping in the wind, each of which he could have pursued. He could have been a political revolutionary. He could have been a national leader. He could have been content to be a teacher and educate minds or to be a physician and heal bodies. But in the end, he chose to be a Savior and save souls.

Anyone near Christ for any length of time heard it from Jesus himself. "The Son of Man came to seek and to save the lost" (Luke 19:10). "The Son of Man did not come to be served, but to serve, and to give his life as a ransom for many" (Mark 10:45).

The heart of Christ was relentlessly focused on one task. The day he left the carpentry shop of Nazareth he had one ultimate aim: the cross of Calvary. He was so focused that his final words were, "It is finished" (John 19:30).

How could Jesus say he was finished? There were still the hungry to feed, the sick to heal, the untaught to instruct, and the unloved ones to love. How could he say he was finished? Simple. He had completed his designated task. His commission was fulfilled. The painter could set aside the brush, the sculptor lay down his chisel, the writer put away his pen. The job was done.

Wouldn't you love to be able to say the same? Wouldn't you love to look back on your life and know you had done what you were called to do?

Our lives tend to be so scattered. We're intrigued by one trend only until the next comes along. Suckers for the latest craze or quick fix. This project, then another. Lives with no strategy, no goal, no defining priority. Playing holes out of order. Erratic. Hesitant. Living life with the hiccups. We are easily distracted by the small things and forget the big things. . . . God wants us to be just like Jesus and have focused lives. (From *Just Like Jesus* by Max Lucado.)

REACTION

7. What does it mean to express your liberty wisely? How did Jesus exercise his freedom?

_____

_____

_____

8. What is the difference between *tolerating* differences and *condoning* wrong behavior?

_____

_____

_____

9. Why is it crucial for believers to love and accept one another? How did Jesus model the approach he expects you to imitate?

_____

_____

_____

10. What characteristics of the world would be different if all Christians lived according to the guidelines in this lesson's Bible passage?

_____

_____

_____

_____

11. How can arguments over controversial issues harm the church?

_____

_____

_____

12. Think of one person to whom you can show greater sensitivity and love. What are some examples you can list of how to do that this week?

_____

_____

_____

LIFE LESSONS

Our freedom is always defined by Christ. Since he gave it to us as a gift, he's the best person to tell us how to use it. He may ask us to use it in ways that surprise us. Those actions may not seem like freedom when they involve saying no to our desires and saying yes to Christ's will for our lives. Some of our greatest moments of freedom come when we choose _not_ to exercise our freedom in order to help someone else.

DEVOTION

Father, help us realize you have truly set us free—free from the lures of status and materialism and peer pressure. Remind us that when the Son sets us free, we are free indeed. And, Father, show us when to sacrifice *our rights out of love for one another. Fill us with your Holy Spirit so our actions build up the church and bring glory to your name.*

JOURNALING

In what ways can you find the balance between enjoying your freedom in Christ and giving up your rights to help others?

FOR FURTHER READING

To complete the book of 1 Corinthians during this twelve-part study, read 1 Corinthians 10:14–11:34. For more Bible passages on Christian freedom, read John 8:31–36; Romans 8:2; Galatians 4:4–5; 5:1–15; and 1 Peter 2:16.

LESSON EIGHT

SPIRITUAL GIFTS

*All these are the work of one and the
same Spirit, and he distributes them
to each one, just as he determines.*
1 Corinthians 12:11

REFLECTION

Think of a role you enjoy fulfilling in your church. Now consider some of the responsibilities others in the church have accepted that benefit you spiritually, and think about the feelings you experience when you are using your abilities to help others. Do you think these are just talents, or is there some more intimate design at work in the church? Why do you think so?

SITUATION

After addressing the believers' responsibilities when it comes to their freedom in Christ, Paul turns to another problem in the Corinthian church. The believers' corporate worship practices had become distorted, chaotic, and dishonoring to God (see 1 Corinthians 11). The church was so splintered, in fact, that it couldn't function as a body in worship. The believers' attitudes in the way the members dressed—and, particularly, in the way they celebrated the Lord's Supper—betrayed deep dysfunctions. In addition, their use of spiritual gifts, which should be a point of strength in the church, had become a point of weakness, confusion, and competition. Paul would now seek to step back and show his readers the big picture of God's gifts.

OBSERVATION

*Read 1 Corinthians 12:1–11 from the New International
Version or the New King James Version.*

NEW INTERNATIONAL VERSION

[1] Now about the gifts of the Spirit, brothers and sisters, I do not want you
to be uninformed. [2] You know that when you were pagans, somehow or
other you were influenced and led astray to mute idols. [3] Therefore I want
you to know that no one who is speaking by the Spirit of God says, "Jesus
be cursed," and no one can say, "Jesus is Lord," except by the Holy Spirit.

[4] There are different kinds of gifts, but the same Spirit distributes
them. [5] There are different kinds of service, but the same Lord. [6] There
are different kinds of working, but in all of them and in everyone it is the
same God at work.

[7] Now to each one the manifestation of the Spirit is given for the
common good. [8] To one there is given through the Spirit a message of
wisdom, to another a message of knowledge by means of the same Spirit,
[9] to another faith by the same Spirit, to another gifts of healing by that
one Spirit, [10] to another miraculous powers, to another prophecy, to
another distinguishing between spirits, to another speaking in different
kinds of tongues, and to still another the interpretation of tongues. [11] All
these are the work of one and the same Spirit, and he distributes them to
each one, just as he determines.

NEW KING JAMES VERSION

[1] Now concerning spiritual gifts, brethren, I do not want you to be ignorant: [2] You know that you were Gentiles, carried away to these dumb
idols, however you were led. [3] Therefore I make known to you that no
one speaking by the Spirit of God calls Jesus accursed, and no one can
say that Jesus is Lord except by the Holy Spirit.

[4] There are diversities of gifts, but the same Spirit. [5] There are differences of ministries, but the same Lord. [6] And there are diversities of

activities, but it is the same God who works all in all. [7] But the manifestation of the Spirit is given to each one for the profit of all: [8] for to one is given the word of wisdom through the Spirit, to another the word of knowledge through the same Spirit, [9] to another faith by the same Spirit, to another gifts of healings by the same Spirit, [10] to another the working of miracles, to another prophecy, to another discerning of spirits, to another different kinds of tongues, to another the interpretation of tongues. [11] But one and the same Spirit works all these things, distributing to each one individually as He wills.

EXPLORATION

1. Why does Paul begin this section by reminding the Corinthians of how they formerly served mute idols? How might this have affected their view on God's spiritual gifts?

_____

_____

_____

_____

2. The Holy Spirit distributes spiritual gifts to all believers. According to this passage, why is there such a variety of gifts?

_____

_____

_____

_____

3. What is the ultimate purpose of spiritual gifts from God? What are some spiritual byproducts that come from the exercise of gifts?

_____

_____

_____

_____

4. Although there are different gifts, there is only one God. Why is that important for us to remember (see also Romans 12:3–8 and Ephesians 4:1–13)?

_____

_____

_____

5. What is your responsibility in regard to your spiritual gifts?

_____

_____

_____

6. If all believers receive spiritual gifts, why do think there are some in the church who feel they have nothing to offer? What are some ways to help other believers identify their gifts?

_____

_____

_____

INSPIRATION

Two of my teenage years were spent carrying a tuba in my high school marching band. My mom wanted me to learn to read music, and the choir was full while the band was a tuba-tooter short, so I signed up. Not necessarily what you would describe as a call from God, but it wasn't a wasted experience either.

I had a date with a twirler.

I learned to paint white shoe polish on school buses.

I learned that when you don't know your music, you need to put your lips to the horn and pretend you do rather than play and remove all doubt.

And I learned some facts about harmony that I'll pass on to you.

I marched next to the bass drum player. What a great sound. *Boom. Boom. Boom.* Deep, cavernous, thundering. At the right measure in the right music, there is nothing better than the sound of a bass drum. *Boom. Boom. Boom.*

And at the end of my flank marched the flute section. Oh, how their music soared. Whispering, lifting, rising into the clouds.

Ahead of me, at the front of my line, was our first chair trumpet. A band member through and through. While some guys shot hoops and others drove hot rods, he played the trumpet. And it showed. Put him on the fifty yard line and let him blow. He could raise the spirit. He could raise the flag. He could have raised the roof on the stadium if we'd had one.

Flute and trumpets sound very different. (See? I told you I learned a lot in band.) The flute whispers. The trumpet shouts. The flute comforts. The trumpet bugles. There's nothing like a trumpet—in limited dosages. A person can only be blasted at for so long. After a while you need to hear something softer. Something sweeter. You need to hear a little flute. But even the sound of the flute can go flat if there is no rhythm or cadence. That's why you also need the drum.

But who wants the drum all by itself? Ever seen a band made up of bass drums? Would you attend a concert of a hundred drums? Probably not. But what band would want to be without a bass drum or flute or trumpet?

The soft flute needs the brash trumpet . . . needs the steady drum . . . needs the soft flute . . . needs the brash trumpet.

Get the idea? The operative word is need. They need each other. By themselves they make music. But together, they make magic.

Now, what I saw two decades ago in the band, I see today in the church. We need each other. Not all of us play the same instrument. Some believers are lofty, and others are solid. Some keep the pace while others lead the band. Not all of us make the same sound. Some are soft, and others are loud. And not all of us have the same ability. Some need to be on the fifty yard line raising the flag. Others need to be in the background playing backup. But each of us has a place. (From *A Gentle Thunder* by Max Lucado.)

REACTION

7. What prevents believers from using their gifts? What explanations or excuses have you heard people use (or used yourself) about not using their gifts?

_____

_____

_____

8. In what ways can believers help one another identify their spiritual gifts?

_____

_____

_____

9. What is one thing you could do this week to share your gifts?

_____

_____

_____

10. What is wrong with saying that some gifts are superior to others?

_____

_____

_____

11. How can you use our gifts in a way that draws attention away from yourself and gives the glory to God?

_____

_____

_____

12. In what ways has this lesson challenged you to change the way you serve in the church?

_____

_____

_____

_____

_____

_____

LIFE LESSONS

Depending on our church background, we may have experienced anything from a complete avoidance of spiritual gifts to an overemphasis on them. We may immediately identify with the "ignorance" about gifts that Paul mentions in 1 Corinthians 12:1. Or we may feel confusion or even fear about gifts because we have seen them misused, misinterpreted, or abused. Paul reminds us that, like all of God's abundance of gifts, spiritual gifts have purposes and uses. They are meant to be part of the glue that holds the body of Christ together. God uses spiritual gifts to meet needs in our lives that we could never meet on our own. Identifying our gifts should increase our sense of responsibility, ministry, and purpose within the body of Christ. Our gifts should never be a reason for pride.

DEVOTION

God, we want only to please you. But fear and anxiety keep us from serving you well. Father, give us the confidence to recognize our spiritual gifts and the courage to use them for your glory. Thank you for the assurance that our imperfect service cannot stand in the way of your amazing power. We give you all the glory for what you accomplish through us.

JOURNALING

In what ways have you personally benefited from the spiritual gifts of others?

FOR FURTHER READING

To complete the book of 1 Corinthians during this twelve-part study, read 1 Corinthians 12:1–11. For more Bible passages on spiritual gifts, read Romans 12:3–8; 1 Corinthians 7:7; 14:1–40; Ephesians 4:11–16; Hebrews 2:4; and 1 Peter 4:10–11.

THE BODY OF CHRIST

*For as the body is one and has many members,
but all the members of that one body, being
many, are one body, so also is Christ. For by
one Spirit we were all baptized into one body.*

1 CORINTHIANS 12:12–13 NKJV

REFLECTION

Unity in the church is something all Christians want but rarely experience. Think of a time when you felt a deep sense of unity among a group of believers. What were the contributing factors to that unity? In what ways were you able to contribute to that sense of unity?

SITUATION

Now that Paul has highlighted the principle of spiritual gifts as given by the Holy Spirit, he can launch into his next major discussion on how those gifts should operate in the church. In this next portion of his letter, which could be described as a "spiritual anatomical lesson" on the body of Christ, Paul stresses that while God gives gifts to certain individuals, the ultimate purpose of those gifts is to benefit the entire body. For this reason, no one should view their gifts as superior to others—for the body of Christ needs *all* the gifts to function properly.

OBSERVATION

Read 1 Corinthians 12:12–26 from the New International Version or the New King James Version.

NEW INTERNATIONAL VERSION
[12] Just as a body, though one, has many parts, but all its many parts form one body, so it is with Christ. [13] For we were all baptized by one Spirit so as to form one body—whether Jews or Gentiles, slave or free—and we

were all given the one Spirit to drink. [14] Even so the body is not made up of one part but of many.

[15] Now if the foot should say, "Because I am not a hand, I do not belong to the body," it would not for that reason stop being part of the body. [16] And if the ear should say, "Because I am not an eye, I do not belong to the body," it would not for that reason stop being part of the body. [17] If the whole body were an eye, where would the sense of hearing be? If the whole body were an ear, where would the sense of smell be? [18] But in fact God has placed the parts in the body, every one of them, just as he wanted them to be. [19] If they were all one part, where would the body be? [20] As it is, there are many parts, but one body.

[21] The eye cannot say to the hand, "I don't need you!" And the head cannot say to the feet, "I don't need you!" [22] On the contrary, those parts of the body that seem to be weaker are indispensable, [23] and the parts that we think are less honorable we treat with special honor. And the parts that are unpresentable are treated with special modesty, [24] while our presentable parts need no special treatment. But God has put the body together, giving greater honor to the parts that lacked it, [25] so that there should be no division in the body, but that its parts should have equal concern for each other. [26] If one part suffers, every part suffers with it; if one part is honored, every part rejoices with it.

NEW KING JAMES VERSION

[12] For as the body is one and has many members, but all the members of that one body, being many, are one body, so also is Christ. [13] For by one Spirit we were all baptized into one body—whether Jews or Greeks, whether slaves or free—and have all been made to drink into one Spirit. [14] For in fact the body is not one member but many.

[15] If the foot should say, "Because I am not a hand, I am not of the body," is it therefore not of the body? [16] And if the ear should say, "Because I am not an eye, I am not of the body," is it therefore not of the body? [17] If the whole body were an eye, where would be the hearing? If the whole were hearing, where would be the smelling? [18] But now God has set the

members, each one of them, in the body just as He pleased. [19] And if they were all one member, where would the body be?

[20] But now indeed there are many members, yet one body. [21] And the eye cannot say to the hand, "I have no need of you"; nor again the head to the feet, "I have no need of you." [22] No, much rather, those members of the body which seem to be weaker are necessary. [23] And those members of the body which we think to be less honorable, on these we bestow greater honor; and our unpresentable parts have greater modesty, [24] but our presentable parts have no need. But God composed the body, having given greater honor to that part which lacks it, [25] that there should be no schism in the body, but that the members should have the same care for one another. [26] And if one member suffers, all the members suffer with it; or if one member is honored, all the members rejoice with it.

EXPLORATION

1. What is the main point that Paul is making in this passage when he compares the body of Christ to a human body?

2. In what ways are the various members of the church dependent on one another?

3. In what ways have you your local church functioning like a human body—with each part depending on each other? How did that serve to bring unity to the church?

_____

_____

_____

4. Paul warns against any part of the body considering itself less important or more important than the others. What kind of parallel behavior in the church does this warn you about?

_____

_____

_____

5. Why did God give more honor to certain parts of the body of Christ?

_____

_____

_____

6. Believers in Christ are to honor one another as parts of the same body. In light of this, how does God want you to treat others in the church?

_____

_____

_____

INSPIRATION

There was some dice-throwing that went on at the foot of the cross. . . . I've wondered what that scene must have looked like to Jesus. As he looked downward past his bloody feet at the circle of gamblers, what did he think? What emotions did he feel? He must have been amazed. Here are common soldiers witnessing the world's most uncommon event, and they don't know it. As far as they're concerned, it's just another Friday morning and he is just another criminal.

"Come on. Hurry up; it's my turn!"

"All right, all right—this throw is for the sandals."

Casting lots for the possessions of Christ. Heads ducked. Eyes downward. Cross forgotten. The symbolism is striking. Do you see it?

It makes me think of us. The religious. Those who claim heritage at the cross. I'm thinking of all of us. Every believer in the land. The stuffy. The loose. The strict. The simple. Upper church. Lower church. "Spirit-filled." Millenialists. Evangelical. Political. Mystical. Literal. Cynical. Robes. Collars. Three-piece suits. Born-againers. Ameners.

I'm thinking of us. And I'm thinking we aren't so unlike those soldiers. (I'm sorry to say.)

We, too, play games at the foot of the cross. We compete for members. We scramble for status. We deal our judgments and condemnations. Competition. Selfishness. Personal gain. It's all there. We don't like what the other did, so we take the sandal we won and walk away in a huff. So close to the timbers, yet so far from the blood.

We are so close to the world's most uncommon event, but we act like common crapshooters huddled in bickering groups and fighting over silly opinions.

How many pulpit hours have been wasted on preaching the trivial? How many churches have tumbled at the throes of miniscuity? How many leaders have saddled their pet peeves, drawn their swords of bitterness, and launched into battle against brethren over issues that are not worth discussing? So close to the cross, but so far from the Christ.

We specialize in "I am right" rallies. We write books about what the other does wrong. We major in finding gossip and become experts in unveiling weaknesses. We split into little huddles and then, God forbid, we split again . . .

Are our differences that divisive? Are our opinions that obtrusive? Are our walls that wide? Is it *that* impossible to find a common cause?

"May they all be one," Jesus prayed. *One.* Not one in groups of two thousand. But one in One. *One* church. *One* faith. *One* Lord. Not Baptist, not Methodist, not Adventist. Just Christian. No denominations. No hierarchies. No traditions. Just Christ.

Too idealistic? Impossible to achieve? I don't think so. Harder things have been done, you know. For example, once upon a tree, a Creator gave his life for his creation. Maybe all we need are a few hearts that are willing to follow suit. (From *No Wonder They Call Him the Savior* by Max Lucado.)

REACTION

7. Why should we resist the temptation to compete with or compare ourselves to other believers (see 2 Corinthians 10:12)?

_____

_____

_____

_____

_____

8. In what ways do petty arguments and divisions in the church tarnish the gospel message?

_____

_____

_____

_____

_____

9. How can believers in Christ learn to appreciate the differences of others in the church instead of allowing them to divide the congregation?

_____

_____

_____

_____

10. What threatens the unity of your local church?

_____

_____

_____

_____

11. What steps can you take to promote peace and harmony in your church?

_____

_____

_____

_____

12. In what ways can you honor someone in your church who may feel unappreciated or insignificant?

_____

_____

_____

_____

LIFE LESSONS

Paul's lesson in anatomy points us in a healthy direction. Our advances in biology and medicine today allow us to marvel at how accurate the illustration proves to be. In fact, if we think about the principles in this passage at the cellular level, its impact deepens. We're almost tempted to think that an organ or an eye could function on its own. But a single cell isolated from the body cannot survive. We need one another. Followers of Jesus face a serious choice. When it comes to our individual relationship with the rest of the body of Christ, the question isn't _if_ we will be involved with the rest of the body but _how_ we will participate in the body.

DEVOTION

Father, we know that disputes and divisions don't belong in the body of Christ. But sometimes we hold on to our hurts, waiting for others to take the first step toward reconciliation. Give us courage, Father, to swallow our pride and reach out in love to our Christian brothers and sisters. Help us to look past our differences and focus on the common ground we share in you.

JOURNALING

Since you're a contributing member of the body of Christ, what can you do to help the body of Christ function most effectively?

FOR FURTHER READING

To complete the book of 1 Corinthians during this twelve-part study, read 1 Corinthians 12:12–31. For more Bible passages on the body of Christ, read Romans 12:4–6; 1 Corinthians 14:4–26; Ephesians 4:25; 5:23–32; and Colossians 1:18, 24–25.

TRUE LOVE

If I speak in the tongues of men or of angels, but do not have love, I am only a resounding gong or a clanging cymbal.

1 CORINTHIANS 13:1

REFLECTION

We use the word *love* in many settings today, and often the meaning can get blurred. But think for a moment how it feels to receive an extravagant present from someone you love. How would you describe that feeling? How does the love between you make it special?

_____

_____

_____

_____

_____

SITUATION

This next section of Paul's letter, widely known as the "love chapter," is among the most recognized passages in the Bible. While it can stand on its own as a beautiful tribute to God's love, Paul actually wrote it as a crucial interlude between sections on the functioning of the body of Christ. In the previous chapter of his letter, and in the one that will follow, Paul discusses the organic nature of this church. But in this chapter—nestled between these two practical bookends—he focuses on the *life* that should permeate the church.

OBSERVATION

Read 1 Corinthians 13:1–13 from the New International Version or the New King James Version.

NEW INTERNATIONAL VERSION

[1] If I speak in the tongues of men or of angels, but do not have love, I am only a resounding gong or a clanging cymbal. [2] If I have the gift of

prophecy and can fathom all mysteries and all knowledge, and if I have a faith that can move mountains, but do not have love, I am nothing. [3] If I give all I possess to the poor and give over my body to hardship that I may boast, but do not have love, I gain nothing.

[4] Love is patient, love is kind. It does not envy, it does not boast, it is not proud. [5] It does not dishonor others, it is not self-seeking, it is not easily angered, it keeps no record of wrongs. [6] Love does not delight in evil but rejoices with the truth. [7] It always protects, always trusts, always hopes, always perseveres.

[8] Love never fails. But where there are prophecies, they will cease; where there are tongues, they will be stilled; where there is knowledge, it will pass away. [9] For we know in part and we prophesy in part, [10] but when completeness comes, what is in part disappears. [11] When I was a child, I talked like a child, I thought like a child, I reasoned like a child. When I became a man, I put the ways of childhood behind me. [12] For now we see only a reflection as in a mirror; then we shall see face to face. Now I know in part; then I shall know fully, even as I am fully known.

[13] And now these three remain: faith, hope and love. But the greatest of these is love.

NEW KING JAMES VERSION

[1] Though I speak with the tongues of men and of angels, but have not love, I have become sounding brass or a clanging cymbal. [2] And though I have the gift of prophecy, and understand all mysteries and all knowledge, and though I have all faith, so that I could remove mountains, but have not love, I am nothing. [3] And though I bestow all my goods to feed the poor, and though I give my body to be burned, but have not love, it profits me nothing.

[4] Love suffers long and is kind; love does not envy; love does not parade itself, is not puffed up; [5] does not behave rudely, does not seek its own, is not provoked, thinks no evil; [6] does not rejoice in iniquity, but rejoices in the truth; [7] bears all things, believes all things, hopes all things, endures all things.

⁸ Love never fails. But whether there are prophecies, they will fail; whether there are tongues, they will cease; whether there is knowledge, it will vanish away. ⁹ For we know in part and we prophesy in part. ¹⁰ But when that which is perfect has come, then that which is in part will be done away.

¹¹ When I was a child, I spoke as a child, I understood as a child, I thought as a child; but when I became a man, I put away childish things. ¹² For now we see in a mirror, dimly, but then face to face. Now I know in part, but then I shall know just as I also am known.

¹³ And now abide faith, hope, love, these three: but the greatest of these is love.

EXPLORATION

1. Based on Paul's opening words in the passage, why is love so important?

_____

_____

_____

_____

_____

2. Why are even the best gifts worthless if they aren't given in love?

_____

_____

_____

_____

3. Paul describes love using words such as *patient, kind, accepting*, and *trusting*. What can you add to that list?

_____

_____

_____

_____

4. What does exhibiting true love require on your part?

_____

_____

_____

5. The love that Paul describes in this passage is selfless and always faithful. Why is it so difficult to demonstrate that kind of love?

_____

_____

_____

6. What does Paul say about the need for spiritual maturity? How does exhibiting the type of love he is discussing lead to possessing that kind of maturity?

_____

_____

_____

INSPIRATION

More than one person has hailed 1 Corinthians 13 as the finest chapter in the Bible. No words get to the heart of loving people like these verses. And no verses get to the heart of the chapter like verses 4 through 8.

"Love is patient, love is kind. It does not envy, it does not boast, it is not proud. It is not rude, it is not self-seeking, it is not easily angered, it keeps no record of wrongs. Love does not delight in evil but rejoices with the truth. It always protects, always trusts, always hopes, always perseveres. Love never fails. But where there are prophecies, they will cease; where there are tongues, they will be stilled; where there is knowledge, it will pass away."

Several years ago, someone challenged me to replace the word _love_ in this passage with my name. I did and became a liar. "Max is patient,

Max is kind. Max does not envy, he does not boast, he is not proud . . ." That's enough! Stop right there! Max is not patient. Max is not kind. Ask my wife and kids. Max can be an out-and-out clod! That's my problem.

And for years that was my problem with this paragraph. It set a standard I could not meet. No one can meet it. No one, that is, except Christ. Does this passage not describe the measureless love of God?

Let's insert Christ's name in place of the word *love* and see if it rings true. "Jesus is patient, Jesus is kind. Jesus does not envy, Jesus does not boast, Jesus is not proud. Jesus is not rude, he is not self-seeking, he is not easily angered, he keeps no record of wrongs. Jesus does not delight in evil but rejoices with the truth. Jesus always protects, always trusts, always hopes, always perseveres. Jesus never fails."

Rather than let this Scripture remind us of a love we cannot produce, let it remind us of a love we cannot resist—God's love.

Some of you are so thirsty for this type of love. Those who should have loved you didn't. Those who could have loved you didn't. You were left at the hospital. Left at the altar. Left with an empty bed. Left with a broken heart. Left with your question, "Does anybody love me?"

Please listen to heaven's answer. God loves you. Personally. Powerfully. Passionately. Others have promised and failed. But God has promised and succeeded. He loves you with an unfailing love. And his love—if you will let it—can fill you and leave you with a love worth giving. (From *A Love Worth Giving* by Max Lucado.)

REACTION

7. What are some things that keep believers from showing their love for others?

_____

_____

_____

_____

8. What can you learn from Christ's example about loving extravagantly and without limits (see Matthew 9:35–36; Mark 8:1–5; and John 11:32–35)?

_____

_____

_____

_____

9. In what ways can God's love free you to love others?

_____

_____

_____

10. How would you describe "unconditional" love? When have you seen that in your life?

_____

_____

_____

_____

11. When are some times that you have seen God's love transform a person?

_____

_____

_____

12. In what ways can you extend God's love to someone else today?

_____

_____

_____

_____

LIFE LESSONS

As we have seen, Paul's words in 1 Corinthians 13 ultimately describes Jesus' love. It is not a love we can easily duplicate. It's a love we experience and then reflect to others. Some of our best moments in life come when we realize that we have been channels of Jesus' love into someone else's life. We are simply passing on to others what was passed on to us.

DEVOTION

Father, the fact you became flesh and dwelt among us proves that you love us far beyond our worth. We ask you, Father, to fill us to overflowing with your love so that it flows freely from us to others. Let our lives be testimonies of your love so that when people look at us, they see a glimpse of your deep love for them.

JOURNALING

What are some ways that you have felt God's love personally?

FOR FURTHER READING

To complete the book of 1 Corinthians during this twelve-part study, read 1 Corinthians 13:1–14:40. For more Bible passages on love, read Matthew 5:43–46; John 13:34–35; Romans 5:5–8; Galatians 5:14; Ephesians 3:16–19; Hebrews 10:24; 1 Peter 1:22; and 1 John 3:11–23.

CHRIST'S VICTORY OVER DEATH

But now Christ is risen from the dead, and has become the firstfruits of those who have fallen asleep. For since by man came death, by Man also came the resurrection of the dead.

1 CORINTHIANS 15:20–21 NKJV

REFLECTION

Human beings can be rather skittish when facing their own mortality. Some people talk about it all the time, while others do everything they can to avoid it. Think about what your friends believe about life after death. What comments have they made when a loved one has died? What conversations have you had with them about death? How do your beliefs differ?

SITUATION

After discussing the nature of God's love, Paul continued his letter by instructing the believers on the logistics and details of worship—and why it was important for them to have order in their gatherings (see 1 Corinthians 14). Now Paul makes a transition back to the heart of his relationship with the Corinthians and the pulse of his ministry, which all rested on the risen Christ. He is aware that certain "teachers" in Corinth have been promoting the idea that there is no resurrection from the dead. Paul realizes that getting it wrong about Jesus' resurrection means getting it wrong about everything else. So, in this next section, he launches into an extended discussion of Jesus' resurrection and its crucial importance to each of us.

OBSERVATION

Read 1 Corinthians 15:20–34 from the New International Version or the New King James Version.

NEW INTERNATIONAL VERSION

[20] But Christ has indeed been raised from the dead, the firstfruits of those who have fallen asleep. [21] For since death came through a man, the resurrection of the dead comes also through a man. [22] For as in Adam all die, so in Christ all will be made alive. [23] But each in turn: Christ, the firstfruits; then, when he comes, those who belong to him. [24] Then the end will come, when he hands over the kingdom to God the Father after he has destroyed all dominion, authority and power. [25] For he must reign until he has put all his enemies under his feet. [26] The last enemy to be destroyed is death. [27] For he "has put everything under his feet." Now when it says that "everything" has been put under him, it is clear that this does not include God himself, who put everything under Christ. [28] When he has done this, then the Son himself will be made subject to him who put everything under him, so that God may be all in all.

[29] Now if there is no resurrection, what will those do who are baptized for the dead? If the dead are not raised at all, why are people baptized for them? [30] And as for us, why do we endanger ourselves every hour? [31] I face death every day—yes, just as surely as I boast about you in Christ Jesus our Lord. [32] If I fought wild beasts in Ephesus with no more than human hopes, what have I gained? If the dead are not raised,

> "Let us eat and drink,
>   for tomorrow we die."

[33] Do not be misled: "Bad company corrupts good character." [34] Come back to your senses as you ought, and stop sinning; for there are some who are ignorant of God—I say this to your shame.

NEW KING JAMES VERSION

[20] But now Christ is risen from the dead, and has become the firstfruits of those who have fallen asleep. [21] For since by man came death, by Man also came the resurrection of the dead. [22] For as in Adam all die, even so in Christ all shall be made alive. [23] But each one in his own order: Christ the firstfruits, afterward those who are Christ's at His coming. [24] Then comes the end, when He delivers the kingdom to God the Father, when He puts an end to all rule and all authority and power. [25] For He must reign till He has put all enemies under His feet. [26] The last enemy that will be destroyed is death. [27] For "He has put all things under His feet." But when He says "all things are put under Him," it is evident that He who put all things under Him is excepted. [28] Now when all things are made subject to Him, then the Son Himself will also be subject to Him who put all things under Him, that God may be all in all.

[29] Otherwise, what will they do who are baptized for the dead, if the dead do not rise at all? Why then are they baptized for the dead? [30] And why do we stand in jeopardy every hour? [31] I affirm, by the boasting in you which I have in Christ Jesus our Lord, I die daily. [32] If, in the manner of men, I have fought with beasts at Ephesus, what advantage is it to me? If the dead do not rise, "Let us eat and drink, for tomorrow we die!"

[33] Do not be deceived: "Evil company corrupts good habits." [34] Awake to righteousness, and do not sin; for some do not have the knowledge of God. I speak this to your shame.

EXPLORATION

1. In this passage, Paul draws a comparison between Adam's death and Christ's death. What did the death of Christ give people that Adam's death did not?

_____

_____

_____

_____

2. What proof do you see that there is life after death?

_____

_____

_____

_____

3. Sin entered the world when humans sinned against God. How will Christ's death eventually destroy sin?

_____

_____

_____

_____

4. Paul's belief in life after death helped him face danger and endure hardship. How does that same belief help you face life? How does it help you face death?

_____

_____

_____

_____

5. Why is Jesus' resurrection from the dead so important in the life of a believer? How should knowing that Jesus was raised from the dead affect the way you live your life?

_____

_____

_____

6. What hope does Christ's resurrection offer to you (see Romans 6:5; Philippians 3:10; and 1 Peter 1:3)?

_____

_____

_____

INSPIRATION

Explorers know that every expedition eventually comes to an end. Vacationers know that no excursion will last forever. Our journey through this life certainly won't.

This heart will feel a final pulse. These lungs will empty a final breath. The hand that directs this pen across the page will fall limp and still. Barring the return of Christ, I will die. So will you.... As the psalmist asked, "Who can live and not see death, or who can escape the power of the grave?" (Psalm 89:48). Young and old, good and bad, rich and poor. Neither gender is spared; no class is exempt. "No one has power over the time of their death" (Ecclesiastes 8:8)....

The finest surgeon might enhance your life but can't eliminate your death. The Hebrew writer was blunt: "People are destined to die once" (Hebrews 9:27). Exercise all you want. Eat nothing but health food, and pop fistfuls of vitamins. Stay out of the sun, away from alcohol, and off drugs. Do your best to stay alive, and, still, you die.

Death seems like such a dead end. Until we read Jesus' resurrection story.... "The angel said to the women, 'Do not be afraid, for I know that you are looking for Jesus, who was crucified. He is not here; he has risen, just as he said'" (Matthew 28:5–6).

He has risen. Three words in English. Just one in Greek: *egerthe.*

So much rests on the validity of this one word. If it is false, then the whole of Christianity collapses like a poorly told joke. Yet, if it is true, then God's story has turned your final chapter into a preface. If the angel was correct, then you can believe this: Jesus descended into the coldest cell of death's prison and allowed the warden to lock the door and smelt the keys in a furnace. And just when the demons began to dance and prance, Jesus pressed pierced hands against the inner walls of the cavern. From deep within he shook the cemetery....

The bodily resurrection means everything. If Jesus lives on only in spirit and deeds, he is but one of a thousand dead heroes. But if he lives on in flesh and bone, he is the King who pressed his heel against the head of death. What he did with his own grave he promises to do with yours: empty it. (From *More to Your Story* by Max Lucado.)

REACTION

7. Why did God send his Son to this earth to die (see Romans 5:6–8; Hebrews 9:27–29; and 1 Peter 2:23–25)?

_____

_____

_____

_____

_____

8. Why is it so important to know from the Gospel accounts that Jesus physically rose from the dead?

_____

_____

_____

_____

_____

9. In what ways is Christ's victory over death essential to your faith?

_____

_____

_____

10. How would your life be different if you *didn't* believe in life after death?

_____

_____

_____

_____

11. What are your thoughts about death? What hope has being a follower of Christ given you as you consider your own mortality?

---

12. How should the truth of this lesson's Bible passage affect the way you live today?

LIFE LESSONS

We might actually describe this passage from Paul as a collection of lessons on death that help us live life. People who deny, dismiss, or downplay the significance of Jesus' resurrection end up without an answer for their own deaths. Pull the resurrection of Jesus out of Christianity, and the result is just another religious system with instructions for people trying to earn their way into God's favor. Those who accept the reality of Jesus' resurrection have good reasons to declare victory over death. Death still has to be faced, but it is a stingless death. Instead of being a cause for dread, death can be a motivation to gratitude. "But thanks be to God, who gives us the victory through our Lord Jesus Christ" (1 Corinthians 15:57 NKJV).

DEVOTION

We praise you, Jesus, for conquering death for us. Your resurrection gives us hope that we will one day rise with you. Until that day, help us to remain faithful. Give us a glimpse into the everlasting so we will live for you no matter what the cost. May we see the joy that is before us, and may we set our hopes on spending eternity with you.

JOURNALING

How can you know for certain that you will one day be raised with Christ?

FOR FURTHER READING

To complete the book of 1 Corinthians during this twelve-part study, read 1 Corinthians 15:1–58. For more Bible passages on Christ's victory over death, see Isaiah 25:7–8; 53:10–12; John 5:24–29; Romans 4:25; 5:12–21; 2 Timothy 1:10; and Hebrews 2:14–15.

LESSON TWELVE

GIVING TO GOD'S WORK

*On the first day of every week, each one of you
should set aside a sum of money in keeping
with your income, saving it up, so that when I
come no collections will have to be made.*

1 CORINTHIANS 16:2

REFLECTION

Think of a time you found great joy in giving to a charity, a church, or even another person. Think about your attitude regarding giving. How has it been a source of blessing to you?

_____

_____

_____

_____

SITUATION

In the book of Acts, we read that the church in Jerusalem was experiencing financial needs. This might have come as a result of the church supporting a large number of widows and others in need (see Acts 6:1–6). It might have come as a result of early believers being cut off from their families. Or it could have been caused by natural setbacks, droughts, and famines in the region (see Acts 11:27–30). Regardless of the reason, Paul was adamant in encouraging the churches throughout the Mediterranean to reach out and help the original church. However, as this next section reveals, Paul realized his previous suggestions and recommendations had to be followed up with specific instructions about giving.

OBSERVATION

Read 1 Corinthians 16:1–11 from the New International Version or the New King James Version.

NEW INTERNATIONAL VERSION
¹ Now about the collection for the Lord's people: Do what I told the Galatian churches to do. ² On the first day of every week, each one of

you should set aside a sum of money in keeping with your income, saving it up, so that when I come no collections will have to be made. [3] Then, when I arrive, I will give letters of introduction to the men you approve and send them with your gift to Jerusalem. [4] If it seems advisable for me to go also, they will accompany me.

[5] After I go through Macedonia, I will come to you—for I will be going through Macedonia. [6] Perhaps I will stay with you for a while, or even spend the winter, so that you can help me on my journey, wherever I go. [7] For I do not want to see you now and make only a passing visit; I hope to spend some time with you, if the Lord permits. [8] But I will stay on at Ephesus until Pentecost, [9] because a great door for effective work has opened to me, and there are many who oppose me.

[10] When Timothy comes, see to it that he has nothing to fear while he is with you, for he is carrying on the work of the Lord, just as I am. [11] No one, then, should treat him with contempt. Send him on his way in peace so that he may return to me. I am expecting him along with the brothers.

New King James Version

[1] Now concerning the collection for the saints, as I have given orders to the churches of Galatia, so you must do also: [2] On the first day of the week let each one of you lay something aside, storing up as he may prosper, that there be no collections when I come. [3] And when I come, whomever you approve by your letters I will send to bear your gift to Jerusalem. [4] But if it is fitting that I go also, they will go with me.

[5] Now I will come to you when I pass through Macedonia (for I am passing through Macedonia). [6] And it may be that I will remain, or even spend the winter with you, that you may send me on my journey, wherever I go. [7] For I do not wish to see you now on the way; but I hope to stay a while with you, if the Lord permits.

[8] But I will tarry in Ephesus until Pentecost. [9] For a great and effective door has opened to me, and there are many adversaries.

[10] And if Timothy comes, see that he may be with you without fear; for he does the work of the Lord, as I also do. [11] Therefore let no one

despise him. But send him on his journey in peace, that he may come to me; for I am waiting for him with the brethren.

EXPLORATION

1. Paul advised the Corinthian church to collect money to support other Christians. In what ways do believers follow this advice today?

_____

_____

_____

_____

2. Paul instructed the Corinthians to save up their offering ahead of time rather than waiting until he came to start collecting. What was the advantage to this plan?

_____

_____

_____

_____

3. Why do think Paul felt the need to be so specific in his instructions regarding giving?

_____

_____

_____

_____

4. What guidelines can you use to know how much money to give to the church (see Leviticus 27:30; Numbers 18:28; 2 Chronicles 31:5–6; and Nehemiah 10:35–38)?

_____

_____

_____

5. Why do you think Paul went out of his way here to explain his travel plans to the Corinthians? What was he trying to communicate to them?

_____

_____

_____

6. Timothy wasn't as prominent as Paul, yet Paul instructed the Corinthians to treat Timothy as an important person. Why does he do this?

_____

_____

_____

INSPIRATION

You don't give for God's sake. You give for your sake. "The purpose of tithing is to teach you to always put God first in your lives" (Deuteronomy 14:23 TLB). In what ways does tithing teach you? Consider the simple act of writing a check or making an online gift. First you enter the date. Already you are reminded that you are a time-bound creature and every possession you have will rust or burn. Best to give it while you can.

Then you enter the name of the one to whom you are giving the money. If the bank would take it, you'd write _God_. But they won't, so you write or type in the name of the church or group that has earned your trust.

Next comes the amount. Ah, this is the moment of truth. You're more than a person with a bank account. You're David, placing a stone in the sling. You're Peter, one foot on the boat, one foot on the lake. You're a little boy in a big crowd. A picnic lunch is all the Teacher needs, but it's all you have.

What will you do? Sling the stone? Take the step? Give the meal? Careful now, don't move too quickly. You aren't just entering an amount ... you are making a confession. A confession that God owns it all anyway.

And then there's the place where you can enter in what your giving is for. Hard to know what to put. It's for the light bills and literature. A little bit of outreach. A little bit of salary.

Better yet, it's partial payment for what the church has done to help you raise your family . . . keep your own priorities sorted out . . . tune you in to his ever-nearness.

Or, perhaps, best yet, it's for you. It's a moment for you to clip yet another strand from the rope of earth so that when he returns you won't be tied up. (From *When God Whispers Your Name* by Max Lucado.)

REACTION

7. What are the purposes of tithing? How do you think it relates to other kinds of giving?

_____

_____

_____

_____

8. Think of a lesson you have learned through giving your money to God's work. Why does giving often result in a learning experience?

_____

_____

_____

9. What are some principles or "rules of the road" that can help you to be a better manager of God's money?

_____

_____

_____

10. Why is financial stewardship so important to God? Where does money or possessions management enter in your relationship with God?

_____

_____

_____

_____

11. Why is it sometimes difficult to give generously to God's work?

_____

_____

_____

_____

12. Think of an improvement you could make, in light of this lesson's Bible passage, in the way you manage your money. How would that improvement change the way you give?

_____

_____

_____

_____

LIFE LESSONS

As stewards of certain possessions and means, we can practice both spontaneous and planned giving. We can be aware of unexpected needs that come up, practicing an attitude that declares we are ready to meet those needs as God supplies. But we can also plan and practice the discipline of systematic giving, including tithing and other giving that relates to ongoing needs. We can commit to supporting a missionary for a set monthly amount, expecting that God will help us meet that commitment. Money is an area in which God clearly tests our obedience, trust, and faithfulness.

DEVOTION

Father, you've been so good to us. Everything we have comes from your gracious hand. Forgive us for clinging too tightly to the things you have given us. Teach us to give generously and sacrificially to your work. Help us to put you first in every area of our lives.

JOURNALING

What does your bank account reveal about your priorities?

FOR FURTHER READING

To complete the book of 1 Corinthians during this twelve-part study, read 1 Corinthians 16:1–24. For more Bible passages on giving to God, read Genesis 28:22; Leviticus 27:30; Deuteronomy 15:10–11; Matthew 22:21; Acts 20:35; Romans 12:6–8; and 2 Corinthians 9:7–15.

LEADER'S GUIDE FOR
SMALL GROUPS

Thank you for your willingness to lead a group through *Life Lessons from 1 Corinthians*. The rewards of being a leader are different from those of participating, and we hope you find your own walk with Jesus deepened by this experience. During the twelve lessons in this study, you will guide your group through selected passages in 1 Corinthians and explore the key themes of the letter. There are several elements in this leader's guide that will help you as you structure your study and reflection time, so be sure to follow along and take advantage of each one.

BEFORE YOU BEGIN

Before your first meeting, make sure the group members have their own copy of the *Life Lessons from 1 Corinthians.* study guide so they can follow along and have their answers written out ahead of time. Alternately, you can hand out the guides at your first meeting and give the group some time to look over the material and ask any preliminary questions. Be sure to send a sheet around the room during that first meeting and have the members write down their name, phone number, and email address so you can keep in touch with them during the week.

There are several ways to structure the duration of the study. You can choose to cover each lesson individually for a total of twelve weeks of discussion, or you can combine two lessons together per week for a total of six weeks of discussion. You can also choose to have the group members read just the selected passages of Scripture given in each lesson, or they can cover the entire book of 1 Corinthians by reading the material listed in the "For Further Reading" section at the end of each lesson. The following table illustrates these options:

Twelve-Week Format

Week	Lessons Covered	Simplified Reading	Expanded Reading
1	The Folly of Human Wisdom	1 Corinthians 1:18–31	1 Corinthians 1:1–31
2	God's Wisdom Revealed	1 Corinthians 2:6–16	1 Corinthians 2:1–16
3	Work That Lasts	1 Corinthians 3:3–15	1 Corinthians 3:1–23
4	Serving Christ	1 Corinthians 4:6–19	1 Corinthians 4:1–6:20
5	Self-Sacrifice	1 Corinthians 9:16–22	1 Corinthians 7:1–9:27
6	Temptation	1 Corinthians 10:1–13	1 Corinthians 10:1–13
7	Liberty and Love	1 Corinthians 10:23–33	1 Corinthians 10:14–11:34
8	Spiritual Gifts	1 Corinthians 12:1–11	1 Corinthians 12:1–11
9	The Body of Christ	1 Corinthians 12:12–26	1 Corinthians 12:12–31
10	True Love	1 Corinthians 13:1–13	1 Corinthians 13:1–14:40
11	Christ's Victory Over Death	1 Corinthians 15:20–34	1 Corinthians 15:1–58
12	Giving to God's Work	1 Corinthians 16:1–11	1 Corinthians 16:1–24

Six-Week Format

Week	Lessons Covered	Simplified Reading	Expanded Reading
1	The Folly of Human Wisdom / God's Wisdom Revealed	1 Corinthians 1:18–31; 2:6–16	1 Corinthians 1:1–2:16
2	Work That Lasts / Serving Christ	1 Corinthians 3:3–15; 4:6–19	1 Corinthians 3:1–6:20

Week	Lessons Covered	Simplified Reading	Expanded Reading
3	Self-Sacrifice / Temptation	1 Corinthians 9:16–22; 10:1–13	1 Corinthians 7:1–10:13
4	Liberty and Love / Spiritual Gifts	1 Corinthians 10:23–33; 12:1–11	1 Corinthians 10:14–12:11
5	The Body of Christ / True Love	1 Corinthians 12:12–26; 13:1–13	1 Corinthians 12:12–14:40
6	Christ's Victory Over Death / Giving to God's Work	1 Corinthians 15:20–34; 16:1–11	1 Corinthians 15:1–16:24

Generally, the ideal size you will want for the group is between eight to ten people, which ensures everyone will have enough time to participate in discussions. If you have more people, you might want to break up the main group into smaller subgroups. Encourage those who show up at the first meeting to commit to attending the duration of the study, as this will help the group members get to know each other, create stability for the group, and help you know how to prepare each week.

Each of the lessons begins with a brief reflection that highlights the theme you will be discussing that week. As you begin your group time, have the group members briefly respond to the opening question to get them thinking about the topic at hand. Some people may want to tell a long story in response to one of these questions, but the goal is to keep the answers brief. Ideally, you want everyone in the group to get a chance to answer, so try to keep the responses to just a few minutes. If you have more talkative group members, say up front that everyone needs to limit his or her answer to two minutes.

Give the group members a chance to answer, but tell them to feel free to pass if they wish. With the rest of the study, it's generally not a good idea to have everyone answer every question—a free-flowing discussion is more desirable. But with the opening reflection question, you can go around the circle. Encourage shy people to share, but don't force them.

Before your first meeting, let the group members know how the lessons are broken down. During your group discussion time the members will be drawing on the answers they wrote to the Exploration and Reaction sections, so encourage them to always complete these ahead of time. Also, invite them to bring any questions and insights they uncovered while reading to your next meeting, especially if they had a breakthrough moment or if they didn't understand something they read.

WEEKLY PREPARATION

As the leader, there are a few things you should do to prepare for each meeting:

- *Read through the lesson.* This will help you to become familiar with the content and know how to structure the discussion times.
- *Decide which questions you want to discuss.* Depending on how you structure your group time, you may not be able to cover every question. So select the questions ahead of time that you absolutely want the group to explore.
- *Be familiar with the questions you want to discuss.* When the group meets you'll be watching the clock, so you want to make sure you are familiar with the Bible study questions you have selected. You can then spend time in the passage again when the group meets. In this way, you'll ensure you have the passage more deeply in your mind than your group members.
- *Pray for your group.* Pray for your group members throughout the week and ask God to lead them as they study his Word.
- *Bring extra supplies to your meeting.* The members should bring their own pens for writing notes, but it's a good idea to have extras available for those who forget. You may also want to bring paper and additional Bibles.

Note that in many cases there will not be one "right" answer to the question. Answers will vary, especially when the group members are being asked to share their personal experiences.

STRUCTURING THE DISCUSSION TIME

You will need to determine with your group how long you want to meet each week so you can plan your time accordingly. Generally, most groups like to meet for either sixty minutes or ninety minutes, so you could use one of the following schedules:

Section	60 Minutes	90 Minutes
WELCOME (members arrive and get settled)	5 minutes	10 minutes
REFLECTION (discuss the opening question for the lesson)	10 minutes	15 minutes
DISCUSSION (discuss the Bible study questions in the Exploration and Reaction sections)	35 minutes	50 minutes
PRAYER/CLOSING (pray together as a group and dismiss)	10 minutes	15 minutes

As the group leader, it is up to you to keep track of the time and keep things moving along according to your schedule. You might want to set a timer for each segment so both you and the group members know when your time is up. (Note that there are some good phone apps for timers that play a gentle chime or other pleasant sound instead of a disruptive noise.) Don't feel pressured to cover every question you have selected if the group has a good discussion going. Again, it's not necessary to go around the circle and make everyone share.

Don't be concerned if the group members are silent or slow to share. People are often quiet when they are pulling together their ideas, and this might be a new experience for them. Just ask a question and let it hang in the air until someone shares. You can then say, "Thank you. What about others? What came to you when you reflected on the passage?"

GROUP DYNAMICS

Leading a group through *Life Lessons from 1 Corinthians* will prove to be highly rewarding both to you and your group members—but that doesn't mean you will not encounter any challenges along the way! Discussions can get off track. Group members may not be sensitive to the needs and ideas of others. Some might worry they will be expected to talk about matters that make them feel awkward. Others may express comments that result in disagreements. To help ease this strain on you and the group, consider the following ground rules:

- When someone raises a question or comment that is off the main topic, suggest you deal with it another time, or, if you feel led to go in that direction, let the group know you will be spending some time discussing it.
- If someone asks a question you don't know how to answer, admit it and move on. At your discretion, feel free to invite group members to comment on questions that call for personal experience.
- If you find one or two people are dominating the discussion time, direct a few questions to others in the group. Outside the main group time, ask the more dominating members to help you draw out the quieter ones. Work to make them a part of the solution instead of the problem.
- When a disagreement occurs, encourage the group members to process the matter in love. Encourage those on opposite sides to restate what they heard the other side say about the matter, and then invite each side to evaluate if that perception is accurate. Lead the group in examining other Scriptures related to the topic and look for common ground.

When any of these issues arise, encourage your group members to follow the words from the Bible: "Love one another" (John 13:34), "If it is possible, as far as it depends on you, live at peace with everyone" (Romans 12:18), and, "Be quick to listen, slow to speak and slow to become angry" (James 1:19).

Thank you again for taking the time to lead your group. May God reward your efforts and dedication and make your time together in this study fruitful for his kingdom.

ALSO AVAILABLE IN THE LIFE LESSONS SERIES

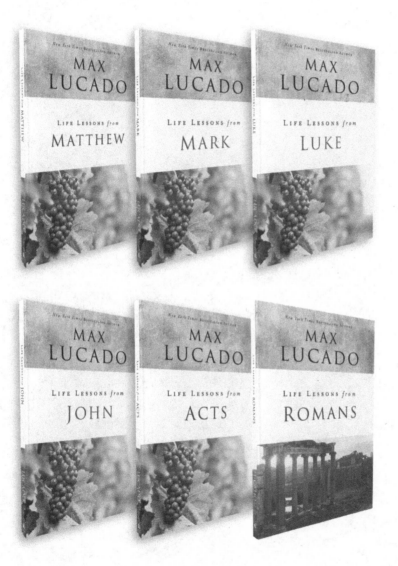